American Data
from the
Records of the High Court
of the
Admiralty of Scotland,
1675–1800

By David Dobson

CLEARFIELD

Printed for
Clearfield Company, Inc. by
Genealogical Publishing Co., Inc.
Baltimore, Maryland
2000

Reprinted for
Clearfield Company, Inc. by
Genealogical Publishing Co., Inc.
Baltimore, Maryland
2006

International Standard Book Number: 0-8063-5025-3

Made in the United States of America

INTRODUCTION

The Admiralty Court was responsible for the civil, criminal and prize jurisdiction of the Lord High Admiral of Scotland as the king's lieutenant and justice general upon the seas. Although the office dates from the mid-fifteenth century, the earliest records date from 1557. In 1681 the Scottish Parliament defined the Court's jurisdiction as extending to *"all maritim and sea-faring causes, forreigne and domestick, whether civil or criminal, whatsoever within this realme, and over all persons as they are concerned in the same."*

The records of the Court have been deposited with the National Archives of Scotland and can be consulted in West Register House, Charlotte Square, Edinburgh. The following abstracts, which have been taken mainly from the court's Register of Decrees, all have some bearing on America and include cases dealing with pirates, privateers, colonial merchants, emigrants, slavers, and seafarers.

The importance of this work is that it identifies the Scots merchants and mariners who were trading with Colonial America and Scottish factors and their servants who often formed the vanguard of subsequent settlement there. An appreciation of trade routes is essential to understanding the pattern of American settlement. Places identified in the book range from Newfoundland to the Gulf of Guinea and from the Baltic to Barbados.

I should like to acknowledge the assistance of Mrs. Sue Mowat, the Scottish Maritime Historian, in the compilation of this work.

Finally the illustration, a document issued to a skipper bound for Guinea and Barbados, appears by kind permission of the Keeper of the Records, the National Archives of Scotland.

David Dobson,
St Andrews,
Scotland. 2000.

Hipped by the Grace of God in good Order and well Conditioned, by *Thomas Thomson*
merch't in Glasgow _____ in and upon the good Ship called the
Hanover Brigantine _____ whereof is Master under God for this present
Voyage *me Gerrit Gerritz* and now riding at Anchor in the
Road of Greenock and by God's Grace bound for *The Coast of Guine___*
_____ to say *fifty six on Boyn, eighty Balls*
&o of in Babadg'e of Sundry Goods & march'de, et g...
. . . afforeid to £D not numbred — on the outer Being
of St. Thomas Thomson & comp___
being marked and numbred as in the Margent, and are to be delivered in the like good Order and well
conditioned, at the aforesaid Port of _____ (the Danger of the Seas only excepted) unto
me alley nhoptburgh furto & on Boace to Ship *according to*
or to *their* Assigns, he or they paying Freight for the said Goods _____

Agreement _____

with Primage and Average accustomed. In witness whereof the Master or Purser of the said Ship hath
affirmed to _____ Bills of Lading, all of this Tenor and Date; the one of which _____ Bills being
accomplished, the other to stand void; And so God send the good Ship to her desired Port in
safety. *Amen.* Dated in *Greenock the Thirtieth of March 1719*

Gerret Gerritz

No 1. to 56

8 of Goods 11c No

AMERICAN DATA FROM
THE SCOTS ADMIRALTY COURT

AC7/4   **undated but after 11 November 1675**

Mr Alexander Murray, now Dean of Killaley in Ireland, V. John Kerr, skipper in Prestonpans

In October 1668, John Kerr, then master of the <u>Star of Peterhead</u>, received from Murray, who was then minister at Harr parish in Virginia, four hogsheads of sweet scented tobacco to be sold in Scotland. Kerr was to have half the proceeds and the rest was to be used to buy linen stockings and coarse woollen cloth, and to indenture a male servant about 15 years old, all to be sent to Virginia on the first ship from Scotland. Kerr did not fulfill this commission, and John Murray, factor for Alexander Murray, cannot get him to repay the money.

AC7/4   **2 November 1677**

James Bogle, John Justine, William Bork, Robert, George and William Boyle, Robert Barns, James Armour, William Napier, James Howat and James Carkett, merchant of Glasgow, and Hugh Boog, writer of Edinburgh V. Joshua Davis, merchant of Bristol.

In 1676 the pursuers imported a large quantity of tobacco from Virginia to Bristol, and employed William Davis and the defender [his son] to declare it at Customs and pay the other expenses on it. They sent him £200 sterling for the purpose, by James Foulis merchant of London. The defender then sent the tobacco to Scotland as requested. As it had been re-exported, £69 4s 4d sterling of the Customs money was refunded, but David has not sent this money to the pursuers.

AC7/4   **2 November 1677**

Charles Charters, merchant of Edinburgh, v. ..... Hilton, widow of Captain William Hilton of New England.

In April 1674 the pursuer consigned goods worth £54 15s 3d sterling to Captain Hilton, to be sold by him in New England. With the proceeds he was to buy ginger and indigo and bring them with him if he returned to Scotland. If he was not returning immediately he was to buy indigo and a few musk skins and give them to Captain Philips to bring to Scotland. Hilton sold the goods, which should have realised £96 15s 3d sterling, but the pursuer has not received any indigo etc. He would have made a profit of £30 sterling on indigo etc in Scotland.

AC7/5   **20 June 1680**

Samuel McReith, merchant of Edinburgh, v. Thomas
Leider, master of the <u>John of London,</u> and Abraham and
Francis Jagart, merchants of London.

In January 1680 the <u>John</u> arrived at Leith to victual for
a voyage to Virginia. McReith supplied Leider with
provisions worth £90 6s 101/2d sterling, for which he
has not paid. The Jagarts, as owners and outredders of
the ship, are also liable for payment of the bill.

AC7/6   **May 20, 1684**

James Armour snr., William Boyle snr., Robert Barnes,
George Boyle, William Napier and James Corbett,
merchant sof Glasgow, and Janet Cunningham, widow
of James Howatt, merchant of Glasgow, Agnes Robb,
widow of John Johnston, merchant of Glasgow, and .....
Brown, widow of Hugh Boick, writer of Edinburgh, v.
William Boick, James and Robert Boyle, merchants of
Glasgow.

In 1675 the pursuers advanced money to the said
William Boick to go to London and buy a cargo for
Virginia from James Foulds , merchant of London, to
sell it in Virginia and buy leaf tobacco. The tobacco
was to be imported to London or a port on the West
Coast of England. Boick shipped the goods to Virginia
on the <u>Elizabeth and Mary of London,</u> master Roger
Newhame. He imported the tobacco to London. As it
was subsequently exported to Scotland, Boick should

have received Customs remission which he should pay to the pursuers, together with the customs duty and freight advanced to him by them .

AC7/7   **January 1686**

Robert Verner v. Sir Robert Baird, John Anderson and John Crawford.

The defenders are partners in a scheme to plant settlers in Carolina, and employed Verner to go there with a shipload of settlers of a Scots colony and plantation then report back to the partners on how the new colony was faring. He is owed £20 2d sterling in wages, plus a half rex dollar per day for time spent ashore at Charleston and 12s Scots per day for board of the boy who was left at Charleston with him.

AC7/7   **26 January 1686**

Thomas Crawford of Carsburn, merchant of Glasgow, v. James, Walter and Ninian Gibson, John Crawford, carpenter of Newark, and George Bentley of Newark and George Lyon.

James Gibson sold Thomas Crawford the <u>Walter of Wairwater</u> with the freight of her last voyage from the West Indies to the Clyde. The defenders are her freighters, who owe:-

4

Walter Gibson: £3222 for freight out and inwards, his own and some he has collected from other freighters

James Gibson, his brother: £10 sterling, freight out and the same inwards

Ninian Gibson, his supercargo: £10 sterling outwards, over and above his portage of 3 tons of goods inwards at £7 sterling per ton

George Lyon, skipper of the ship: £1148 freights collected by him

James Wardroper: £720 freight of goods and servants out and inwards, plus the freight outwards of a blackamoor boy belonging to William Colquhoun

John Crawford: £600 for his passage, and freight of goods out and inwards

George Bentley: £84 for his passage, and freight of goods out and inwards

Alexander Crawford: £84 for freight of goods out and inwards

George Bentley, Ninian Gibson, and Alexander Crawford: £60 for one Hundredweight of gunpowder taken from the ship and £200 for lead.

AC7/7   **6 April 1686**

Patrick Crawford, mariner of Edinburgh, v. Sir Robert Baird of Sauchtonhall, William Lockhart and Charles Charters, merchants of Edinburgh, Alexander Reid snr, goldsmith of Edinburgh, and Sir Alexander Gilmour of Craigmillar

The defenders are some of the partners in a scheme to make plantations in Carolina. They agreed on 15 September 1682 with their trustees Sir John Cochran of Ochiltree and Sir George Campbell of Cessnock jnr., to lend money to Sir Robert Baird their cashier to be given to several persons to go to Carolina with servants and goods, to settle the said plantation and report back to the Undertakers of the project. As the pursuer has been in America previously, he was hired by baillie Charles Charters at £5 sterling per month "to view the whole country, of what soil and nature it was of and what it did or could bear and produce, and to make a faithful report thereof to the said undertakers". He sailed from the Clyde on 26 September 1682 and returned on 4 July 1683, having discharged his commission and made a map of the colony. He is still owed £546 Scots in wages and expenses.

AC7/8   **15 April 1687**

Walter Gibson, merchant of Glasgow, v. George Lyon, skipper of Glasgow.

Intending to settle a plantation in Carolina, in 1684 the pursuer commissioned Lyon and Mr William Dunlop to inspect land at Port Royal, along with Gibson's brother James, and if they could 'hold the bargain made with the Proprietors' to take 12,000 acres, to be divided with Mr Dunlop in proportion with the number of settlers each party had. Each settler was to have 50 acres for 2d sterling per acre per year. George Lyon shipped 14 servants with goods and provisions for settling the plantation in the <u>Carolina Merchant</u>,master James Gibson. On arrival at Charleston, Lyon sold the servants and goods without attempting to settle the plantation. Mr Dunlop settled his servants at Port Royal. The pursuer has lost £500 sterling, which he would have made if Lyon had settled a plantation as ordered.

AC7/9   August 21, 1691

James Knight, sole owner, and Thomas Curtis, master, of the <u>Whiling Wind [alias] the Endeavour of Weymouth</u> v. Robert Stewart of Eday and Gilbert Dick of Leith present pretended master.

On her return from a voyage to Virginia, the ship was taken by a French privateer and a few days later retaken by a Dutch man-of-war belonging to the Company of the Great Fishery of South Holland. The captain of the man-of-war left the <u>Endeavour</u> in the custody of Andreas Bruce of Broadsound in Shetland. Curtis got the owners of the Dutch fishery company to agree that his ship was not a lawful prize, as she had been in the possession of the French.

AC7/10/175-179   **May 22, 1703**

Kenneth Bayne, a merchant in Edinburgh, v. William Troup, a merchant in London, for money owing on some stock ventured with a Mr Guthrie of Dundee to Maryland

AC7/10/644-658   **October 27, 1703**

James Graham, late baillie of Edinburgh, v. Thomas Hamilton of Olivestob, for payment of £19,000 Scots money as his half of the value of two cargoes of tobacco shipped for them from Maryland by William Dorwall on board the <u>Hopewell</u>, formerly the <u>Rebecca</u>, and the <u>John and Hester</u>.

AC7/11/1326-1357   **November 7, 1704**

Andrew Cockburn, cashier to the Company of Scotland trading to Africa and the Indies, v. David Drummond of Cultmalundie, James Brown snr., an apothecary in Edinburgh, David Lander, deacon of the Cordiners of the Canongate, Agnes Campbell, widow of Andrew Andreson, printer in the Canongate, Alexander Douglas, John Fobres, Major John Forbes, Patrick McDougall, William Wilson, David Plenderleith, James Robertson, Mrs Patricia Ruthven, Mary Rymer, Thomas Whyte, William Wightman skinner jnr., David Whyte, for

subscriptions due on stock purchased in the afore mentioned company.

AC7/12/994-1014   **July 3, 1705**

Isaac Fallafield, merchant in Cockermouth, Cumberland, England, v. David Ferguson, skipper in Ayr, John and Robert Minors, merchants and late provosts of Ayr.

The Lyon on a voyage to the West Indies and return was cast away on the coast of Ireland, whereupon the sugar and other goods saved were sold or disposed of by David Ferguson, master of the said ship. The interest of Matthias Partis and John Wolsy, co-partners with the Minors, in this cargo was assigned to the pursuers.

AC7/12/1117-1123   **August 14, 1705**

Andrew Cockburn, cashier to the African and Indian Company of Scotland, v. Richard Harvieson, writer in Edinburgh, George Turnbull, Writer to the Signet, and John Turnbull, merchant in Edinburgh, for subscriptions die on stocks purchased in the above company.

AC7/12/1197-1201, 1201-1213, 1373-1496
         September 17, 1705

Roderick McKenzie, secretary to the Company of Scotland trading to Africa and the Indies, as factor for and in the name of the said company, and Alexander Higgins, procurator fiscal of the High Court of the

Admiralty, for his interest v. Captain Thomas Green, commander of the <u>Worcester</u>, Captain John Madder, chief mate, and John Reynolds, second mate.

AC7/13/1076-1102   **August 30, 1706**

Andrew Cockburn, cashier to the Company of Scotland trading to Africa and the Indies v. David Kennedy, Thomas Warrender, George Seaton, Thomas Spense, John Watson jnr., Gilbert More, John Schaw snr., Alexander Anstruther, Walter Dennistoun, Lieutenant Gilbert Hall, Benjamin Harrison (in James County, Virginia), Robert Keith, Alexander Stevenson, Captain John Stewart, William Thomson, John Maxwell, John Kyle, Robert Pollock, William McTaggart, William Smith, and Patrick Herron, for payments due on subscriptions made for stock in the above-mentioned company.

AC7/13 & 14   **October 2, 1706**

Thomas Guybon, a merchant in London, and William Drummond, a writer in Edinburgh, his factor, v. the Directors and managers of the Company of Scotland trading to Africa and the Indies, for themselves and in the name and behalf of the said company, Thomas Lockhart, surveyor in Leith, John Jameson, carpenter, Sir Robert Blackwood, merchant in Edinburgh and one of the directors of the said company, Captain James Miller, master of the <u>Hannah Galley</u>, ... Burgers, chief mate thereof, and John Ainsworth, merchant in London.

Thomas Guybon brings an action to collect money on a bond given to him by John Ainsworth, who owns the <u>Hannah Galley</u>, which is employed in the service of the Company of Scotland trading to Africa and the Indies.

AC7/16/463-498   **July 11, 1710**

Margaret Gibb, widow of George Mossman v. William Dalling, skipper in Bo'ness, 'for value of goods lost in the Darien Expedition'.

AC7/16/1064-1071   **December 15, 1710**

James Graham, v. Roderick McKenzie, former secretary to the Company of Scotland trading to Africa and the Indies. James Graham was master of the <u>Dolphin</u>, one of the ships of the Company of Scotland trading to Africa and the Indies. He had been taken as a prisoner to Carthagena and wanted damages from the Company's 'dead stock'.

AC7/17/270-275   **July 3, 1711**

George Gray, a carpenter in Leith, hired by Archibald Galbraith, skipper and master of the <u>Friendship of Leith</u>, for £3 sterling per month, claiming wages for a voyage from Leith to Maryland and back.

AC7/17/352-362   **August 8, 1711**

Robert Stewart, James Brabner, George Fordyce, merchants in Aberdeen, owners of the ship formerly called the <u>Joanna</u> and now the <u>Virginia Merchant of Aberdeen,</u> master Alexander Inglis, and John Innes, writer in Edinburgh, their factor, v. Captain William Colyier of <u>HMS Mermaid</u>, who had rescued their ship from a French privateer when on a voyage to Virginia, and wanted to keep the cargo.

AC7/17/537-540   **December 14, 1711**

John Harrison and Joseph Edgar v. William Roe for £100, the value of goods furnished for a voyage and cargo to and from the West Indies in 1709. John Shepherd, James Black, and William Rae were partners in a society for buying and selling tobacco and other sea-borne goods, and in the cargoes of the <u>Amity</u> and the <u>Patience</u>.

AC7/17/825-835   **August 12, 1712**

Dr James Crawford of Lochevat v. Edmonstone of Ednam. Two years before, at Port Royal, Jamaica, Crawford entrusted to Edmonstone two bottles of cidron water and a gold guinea worth respectively £28 and £12 18s Scottish money, and would now like repayment.

AC10/120 1712

Petition for Samuel McCaull, John Tod, and Thomas Smith, merchants of Glasgow. They raised a petition against John Hamilton, a merchant of Whitehaven, England, for non-fulfilment of an agreement to make a Charter Party with John Golding, master of the Centurion of Whitehaven for a voyage to Virginia. Having heard that Hamilton is about to leave the country they ask that he be imprisoned.

AC8/139 1712

John Finlayson, master of the Beattie of Bo'ness v. her owners for their share of the losses on two voyages, one from Greenock to Sweden and the other from Greenock to Antigua, valued at £5092 Scots.

AC/7/19/9-15 January 19, 1714

Michael Wallace, merchant in Glasgow, v. Patrick Jameson, ship-mate in Bo'ness. Robert Gregory for Wallace, put on board Jameson's ship the Euphan, 9 hogsheads of Virginia leaf tobacco to be delivered to James Murieson in Amsterdam. Delivery not being made, action is brought for the value of the tobacco, the expense of making enquiries concerning it, and interest on his money, viz. £1169 19 shillings, £12, £130, in all £1311 19 shillings Scots.

AC7/18/188-198   **April 1, 1713**

John Mowbray v. James Craigie. Lawrence Craigie, deceased, brother of James, accepted from John Mowbray a certain sum of money with which to buy 333 pound weight of Virginia leaf tobacco for the use of Mowbray in Norway. After his brother's death, James paid for one third of the tobacco, and the action is brought for the amount still due.

AC8/196   **1715**

Charles Dalrymple, merchant in Glasgow, executor and creditor of the late Fergus Cathcart, son of the late Robert Cathcart of Greenock, v. John, Robert, Margaret and ...., brothers and sisters of the late Fergus for the proceeds of goods imported from Barbados in the galley <u>Anna of Glasgow</u>, master James Barclay.

AC7/21/550-599   **July 31, 1716**

Antony Whyteside of Whitehaven Cumberland, England, v. John Bogle, merchant in Glasgow, for undue delay in a voyage of the <u>Mary Galley of Whitehaven</u> from Whitehaven to Virginia or Maryland and return with a cargo of tobacco.

AC8/199   1716

Petition from Thomas Crawford, a cabinetmaker in Leith, acting for Mr Samuel Russell and Company, linen drapers of London. Russell's apprentice Robert Sherwine had absconded with goods worth £1200 sterling, now known as Robert Burden together with another runaway apprentice ...... Scott or Johnston, have signed on with Captain Young, a shipmaster of Burntisland, for passage to Virginia. Crawford petitions for their arrest.

AC9/574   1716

Antony Whiteside in Whitehaven, Cumberland, England, master and part-owner of the galley <u>Mary of Whitehaven</u> and his factor William Whiteside v. John Bogle, merchant of Glasgow, for the freight of Virginian tobacco. Reference to Gilbert McMichan, supercargo, George Scott, surveyor in Greenock, Arthur Park, merchant in Greenock, Joseph Tucker, carpenter in Greenock, Richard Benn, mariner in Whitehaven, John Baird, merchant in Glasgow, Robert Bogle, merchant in Glasgow, David Graham of Orchell, Customs Controller of Port Glasgow, John Mure, Customs Controller of Port Glasgow, Joseph Pearson in Whitehaven carpenter on the <u>Mary,</u> and Thomas Mathewson, mariner in Whitehaven sailor on the <u>Mary</u>.

AC9/584   **1716**

Arthur Tran, merchant in Glasgow, v. Robert Arthur,
master of the <u>Fortune of Glasgow</u> re a cargo of sugar
from Antigua. Reference to Andrew Leitch, merchant in
Glasgow, William Eccles, skipper in Greenock, William
Arthur, mariner in Crawfordyke, John Miller, carpenter
in Greenock, John Bogle, merchant in Glasgow,
Alexander Watson, carpenter in Newark, Charles
Menzies, carpenter in Newark, Claud Henderson,
merchant in Glasgow, James Peadie, jnr., merchant in
Glasgow, David Graham of Orchall, customs collector in
Port Glasgow, John Moor, customs collector in Port
Glasgow.

AC13/1/160   **1716**

Instrument of protest. "I Alexander Spotswood, HM
Lieutenant Governor and Commander in Chief of the
Colony and Dominion of Virginia, do make known and
manifest that on the twentyfifth day of July in the fifth
year of the reign of our Sovereign Lord George, by the
Grace of God King of Great Britain, France and Ireland,
Defender of the Faith, Anno Domini 1715, personally
appeared before me William Whiteside, master of the
good ship called the <u>Mary of Whitehaven</u> which now
rides at anchor in the River of Rappachannick within
this colony, and exhibited copy of a charter party of
affreightment, made between Anthony Whyteside,
owner of the said ship, and John Bogle of the City of
Glasgow of North Britain, merchant ...". The charter
party stated that within 90 days of his arrival in Virginia,

William Whiteside would unload the outward cargo and reload with tobacco, "excepting room for the reasonable priviledge of portage for the Master, Mate and men ...". If the ship was detained longer than 90 days, John Bogle was to pay 40 shillings sterling "demurrage". The ship has now been detained for more than 90 days because John Bogle's factor has not yet loaded her with tobacco. Whiteside gave notice to the factor who said he had orders to detain the ship until the next crop if it was not loaded sooner. So Whiteside "doth hereby protest against the freighters of the said ship ... for the demurrage in the charter party aforesaid for all the time she shall be obliged to stay, over and above the said ninety days ... as well as for all damage the ship and ship's company may sustain by reason of their being detained beyond the tie limite in the said charter party". At Williamsburg, Virginia, 17 August 1716.

AC7/22/440-478   August 17, 1717

George Gray, merchant in Glasgow, v. Robert Arthur, skipper in Crawfordsdyke. Arthur, as master of the Fortune of Glasgow, undertook for Gray, the sole freighter of the ship in 1715, a voyage from Port Glasgow to Antigua and return. In Antigua Charles Dunbar and James Watson shipped on board 3 hogsheads of sugar which was damaged by water on the voyage. Action is taken for the value of the spoiled sugar.

AC9/595   **1717**

George Gray, merchant in Glasgow, v. Robert Arthur, master of the <u>Fortune of Glasgow</u> concerning a cargo of sugar from Antigua. Reference to Charles Dunbar, James Watson, Arthur Tran, merchant in Glasgow, James Corbett jnr., merchant in Glasgow, John Hay, merchant in Glasgow, Robert Arthur, merchant in Glasgow, George Houstoun, merchant in Glasgow, George Daniel, merchant in Glasgow, James Barclay, shipmaster in Crawfordyke.

AC16/1   **November 4, 1718**

Roger Hows, John Clerk, Richard Jones, John Eshwell, William Fenton, Hayman Saturley, William Minty, William Green, John Jarret, Thomas Dowden, John Stewart, James Saul, Richard Luntly, Thomas Roger, Nicolas Kerny, Dennis Jophen, Henry Thixton, late sailors on the <u>Eagle,</u> now prisoners in Edinburgh Castle accused of piracy, involving the <u>Burk</u>, Captain Brisk, and another unnamed ship Captain Porter. The accused had sailed to Hispaniola and along the American coast where they captured a French sloop which was taken to Privateer Bay where Howell Davies was appointed of the <u>Burk</u>. They then sailed to Cuba and attacked a ship from Philadelphia. At Cape Franbaway in Hispaniola they plundered two French ships, a schooner from New England, a sloop from the Isle of Providence, a French ship from Curacao, and a New York vessel, before they landed at the Island of May. Next they captured ships

from Antigua, Liverpool and Barbados. The Liverpool
ship was renamed the <u>Royal James</u> which they sailed to
the River Gambia on the Coast of Guinea. There they
plundered a fort and took a sloop belonging to
Barbados. Next they moved on to Bance Island where
they plundered and burnt two English ships and a Scots
vessel commanded by Mr Auchenleck. Another Scots
ship, commanded by Captain Graham was plundered as
was an Ostend ship, a Dutch ship [renamed the <u>Royal
Rover</u>], before they attacked some English ships at
anchor off Annanbao. After that they left for Brazil and
the West Indies. Later they took a snow the <u>Eagle of
New York</u>, Captain McIntosh, and headed across the
Atlantic, en route they attacked another vessel a New
Englander bound for Barbados, before they landed on
the west coast of Scotland. The pirate ships were under
the command of Captain Davies, Captain Roberts and
Captain Kennedy. At their trial in Edinburgh the
witnesses included Duncan Daw and Peter Cheap.
Duncan Daw, mate to Duncan Glasford, shipmaster in
Bo'ness, aged 32, married, was serving on board the
<u>Edward and Sarah of Barbados</u>, master James Nisbet,
on a trading voyage along to Coast of Guinea heading
for the River Sorralou when they were boarded by the
pirates who took gold, 'elephants teeth' and some
negroes. Peter Cheap, supercargo on the <u>Loyalty of
Glasgow</u>, aged 27, unmarried, was on a trading voyage
from Europe to the Coast of Guinea when they were
attacked by the pirates on 26 May 1719.

They were all found guilty and sentenced to be hung at
Leith Sands in January 1721.

AC9/626   **1718**

William Menzies, a merchant in London, v. Sir Alexander Anstruther of Newark for freight on the <u>Margaret of Leith</u>, master Ebenezer Hathorn, on a voyage to the West Indies. Reference to John Hampton a supercargo, Lewis Hary, and Alexander Davidson a shipmaster.

AC7/23/100-117; 26/908-967   **April 4, 1719**

Charles Ramsay, merchant, v. George Beattie, merchant, Robert Burnet, Thomas Burnet, Robert Gentleman [a relative of David Gentleman deceased], Henry Straton and George Chapland, merchants in Jamaica and executors of the estate of David Gentleman, re the auction and sale of the <u>Elizabeth of Montrose</u>.

David Gentleman, as master of the <u>Elizabeth of Montrose</u>, for Ramsay part owner of the said vessel, made several voyages to foreign countries, particularly the West Indies, from 16 March 1716 to 30 November 1717, when he died in Jamaica. Neither Gentleman, during his lifetime, nor his executors since made any account or return of profits of these voyages, for which action is now brought. The amount of these profits less necessary deductions is £719 sterling.

AC9/647   **1719**

Charles Ramsay, a merchant of Montrose, part-owner of
the <u>Elizabeth of Montrose</u> v. George Beattie, a
merchant in Montrose, and the other owners of the said
ship for payment of a bill of bottomry. The late master,
David Gentleman, died in Jamaica, and Andrew Ford, a
mariner in Kingston, Jamaica, took over command, and
the bottomry was advanced to him by George Chaplain
and Henry Straton, merchants in Jamaica. Refers to
Thomas Burnet of Glenbervie, his brother Robert
Burnet, Sir Alexander Ramsay of Balmain, James Blair,
a merchant in Edinburgh, Alexander and George
Auchterlony, merchants in London, and Robert
Gentleman, a merchant in Montrose.

AC7/24/710-779   **August 30, 1720**

Robert Jackson, mariner and master of the
<u>Confirmation of Workington</u>, in Cumberland, England,
and Michael Heelkeld, currier in Whitehaven,
Cumberland, his factor, v. John McFarland, George
Craig, Andrew Buchanan, and John Mitchell, merchants
in Glasgow, and John Govan of Mains, for failure to pay
the hire of the ship on a voyage to the West Indies and
American colonies.

AC9/691   **1720**

Robert Jackson, master of the <u>Confirmation of
Workington</u> in Cumberland, England, v. John McFarlane

and Robert Govan, merchants in Glasgow, regarding a voyage to Virginia in 1717. Reference to the crew of the <u>Confirmation</u> - John Mason and Daniel Kitchen from Whitehaven, George Egglesfield, Jeremiah Bowman, Joseph Jackson, and John Fletcher from Ellenborough, William Mason from Windscale, Michael Howard from Harrington, and Robert Steel from Workington; also to John Mason, mariner in Whitehaven, and the crew of the <u>Pearl of Whitehaven</u>, George Weir, shipmaster in Crawfordyke, James Dennie, mariner in Crawfordsdyke, George Craig merchant in Glasgow, James McBrayer mariner in Glasgow, James Guthrie merchant in Glasgow, James Robertson merchant in Glasgow, John Charters merchant in Glasgow, Patrick Buchanan merchant in Glasgow, Hugh Black merchant in Glasgow, Robert Alexander merchant in Glasgow, Anthony Walker master of the <u>Brotherhood of Whitehaven</u>, Samuel McCou mariner in Gourrock, James McNeir merchant in Stirling, John Bogle writer in Edinburgh, and John Calder and Company in London.

AC7/24/958-978   October 14, 1720

Alexander Duff of Drummore, William Fraser, a merchant in Inverness, Alexander McIntosh of Wester Drakes, James Dunbar, merchant in Inverness, and Alexander Tolmie, merchant in Fortrose, all part owners of the <u>Ann galley of Inverness</u> and George Roger as having right by commission by them v. Isobel Dawling, sister of James Dawling, skipper, deceased, Isaac Wyber, schoolmaster, her husband, and John Jerbie, shipmaster in Queensferry, for freight money owing.

Account of debursements on voyages to Virginia, the West Indies and elsewhere.

AC16/1/316-400   **November 1, 1720**

Roger Flows and other charged with piracy and murder against several vessels in the West Indies in 1720. Ten of them found guilty and sentenced to be hanged at Leith within the flood-mark.

AC9/712   **1720**

John Walker, merchant in Cockermouth, v. John Wair snr and jnr., and others, merchants in Glasgow, re a voyage to Maryland. Reference to the Commissioners of Somerset County, Maryland, John Jones, Thomas Dishell snr., Captain Charles Ballard, Captain Nicolas Evans, and Joseph McCloster; Robert Graham, George Currie, Robert Thomson, John Buchanan, and 'Bristol John' Robertson snr., all merchants in Glasgow; Thomas Lutewadge and Clement Nicholson, merchants in Whitehaven.

AC9/713   **1720**

Robert Strachan, carpenter, and other crew members of the <u>Christian of Leith</u>, v. Alexander Hutton, re unpaid wages, Hutton claims that they mutinied in Barbados. Reference to the crew of the <u>Christian</u> – Harry White, bosun, David Buchan, James Colman, Andrew

McIlwraith, John Barclay, and William Burne; Robert Robertson merchant in Glasgow, Duncan Daw mariner in Bo'ness, James Liddel supercargo, David Rutheford a merchant in Edinburgh, David Mitchell a gardener at St Antony's and his wife Janet Gunnance, Thomas Edgar, surgeon apothecary in Edinburgh and his son Mr John Edgar.

AC9/718   **1720**

John Daniel, cooper on the <u>Loyalty of Glasgow</u>, master Mungo Graham, v. Richard Graham, a merchant in Glasgow, re wages unpaid on a voyage to Guinea and Virginia when he was captured by pirates. Reference to William Anderson, a merchant in Glasgow, John Bogle, a merchant in Glasgow, and David Alexander, surgeon on the <u>Loyalty</u>.

AC9/714   **1720**

Colonel William Wanton and Captain Edward Thurston, merchants in Newport, Rhode Island, and their factors Robert Partridge, a merchant in London, and Robert Pringle, a writer in Edinburgh, v. Andrew Fulton, master of the 70 ton sloop <u>Queen of Newport</u> [built in Tiver Town, Massachusetts]. Fulton received goods to be delivered to Mr Richard Harris in Curacao but went to Jamaica instead and sold them and the ship in Port Royal. He is now in Leith with his brother and uncle. Reference to Samuel Cranston, Governor of Rhode Island, Oliver Kennedy, Richard Partridge, Captain Philip

Wanton, commander of the sloop <u>Friendship of Rhode Island</u>, Dr William Fulton in New Bristol, New England father of Andrew Fulton, and John McKenzie a goldsmith in Port Royal.

Bond of Caution, 1719. Alexander McCulloch, a merchant in Edinburgh, master of the Stocking Manufactory opposite the main guard of Edinburgh, becomes caution that Andrew Fulton, merchant in Leith, will appear at all diets brought against him by the following, and stay in the house of Edward Cutler a writer in Edinburgh. Reference to William Wanton in Newport, Rhode Island, Edward Thurston in Newport, Rhode Island, Richard Pearsting, a merchant in London, and Robert Pringle, a writer in Edinburgh.

AC9/702   **1720**

Cases involving the voyage of the <u>Anne of Inverness</u> from Inverness via Cork to Barbados and Virginia in 1716. Reference to James Dalling, shipmaster of South Queensferry, commander of the galley <u>Anne of Inverness.</u>

AC7/25 & 26   **March 10, 1721**

Patrick Inglis, writer in Edinburgh, v. James Graham of Kilmannan, Admiral Depute of the Western Seas, and James Campbell of Stonefield, Sheriff Depute.

Roger Hews and other sailors of the <u>Eagle</u> snow, through their pursuer, Inglis, bring an action to recover, from their effects which had been seized, sufficient funds to pay the lawyers engaged to defend them at their trial on a charge of piracy. The snow began life as the <u>Eagle of New York</u>, sent with provisions to Barbados, but was caught on the way by pirates.

AC7/25/822-827   July 28, 1721

Thomas Coates, a merchant in Whitehaven, Cumberland, England, and other owners of the ship the <u>Mary and Francis of Whitehaven</u>, and Captain Isaack Langtoun, their factor, v. Arthur Tran and Robert Robertson, merchants in Glasgow, who had hired a ship for a voyage to Virginia and had kept it longer than agreed.

AC7/25/946-975   August 22, 1721

David Alexander, late surgeon on the <u>Loyalty of Glasgow</u>, v. Richard Graham, William Anderson, and John Bogle, merchants in Glasgow, for non-payment of wages. The <u>Loyalty</u> had taken slaves from Guinea to Barbados but the ship had been attacked by pirates. Witnesses of the piracy had gone to Virginia or Maryland where it was difficult to reach them because of irregular postal services. According to accounts sent by Mr Alexander Dundas, the defenders' factor in Barbados, there were upwards of fifty slaves belonging

to the cargo of the <u>Loyalty</u> unloaded at Bridgetown, Barbados, and disposed of there for the defender.
AC9/769   1721

David Alexander, former surgeon on the <u>Loyalty of Glasgow</u>, master Patrick Cheap, v. her freighters in a slaving voyage to the coast of Guinea and the West Indies, for his wages. The ship was captured by pirates on her way home.

Reference to Daniel Cooper, Alexander Carstairs, merchants in Amsterdam, Gavin Cathe, mate on the <u>Loyalty of Glasgow</u>, Alexander and Charles Dundas, merchants in Barbados, Richard Graham, William Anderson and John Bogle, merchants in Glasgow.

AC9/769   January 3, 1721

Alexander Gordon, late surgeon on the <u>Loyalty of Glasgow</u>, master Patrick Cheape, v. Richard Graham, William Anderson, and John Bogle, merchants in Glasgow, re a voyage scheduled from Glasgow via Liverpool and Rotterdam to Guinea, returning to the Clyde via Barbados and Virginia. Alexander Gordon had served as surgeon from 2 August 1718 to 28 May 1719.

Reference to Barnet St John, Edward Charnley, William and Antony McChiere, Philip Jones, Roselle Arrowsmith, Richard Hardie, David Gavin Carter mate, William Shearer, David Alexander doctor, Thomas Brewer, ... Layton, Clem Humbley, Alexander and Charles Dundas factors in Barbados; Captain Maxwell, Dr William

Paterson, Captain William Ballentyne, William Cooper, David Arnott and Christopher Carmichael all in Barbados; John Daniel cooper, David Alexander surgeon on the Loyalty; John Carstairs in Rotterdam; depositions of witnesses being taken in Virginia; and being captured by pirates on 6 May 1719.

AC7/26/681-823   March 30, 1722
AC9/849   1722

John Stenhouse, commander of the Catherine of Whitehaven, and his factor John Binning, a writer in Edinburgh, v. James Wallace and Arthur Park, merchants in Greenock, who had hired the ship in 1718 for a voyage to Virginia or Maryland, and had not paid sufficiently for freight, damage and demurage.

Reference to John Watson, merchant in Glasgow and supercargo on the Thomas, Henry Benn mate on the Katherine, Lancelot Forester and Robert Benn of the crew of the Katherine, Thomas Blair supercargo of the Integrity of Whitehaven, Adam Bald supercargo on the Thomas of Whitehaven, and Nathanial Walker, master of the Thomas, and various merchants in Glasgow, Belfast, and Whitehaven.

AC7/27/2186-2199   December 28, 1722

Robert Brown, John Dickson, and Samuel Chiesly, merchants in Glasgow, v. William Robertson, now master of the Albany, whom they had employed as a

supercargo on a voyage to Virginia. The supercargo
had taken a great deal on himself as he had bought a
ship with his employers' money without permission, and
had refused to give an account of any of this.

AC8/285   **1722**

Robert Brown, John Dickson and Samuel Chiesly,
merchants in Glasgow, v. William Robertson, merchant
in Glasgow, who they employed as supercargo on the
<u>Drummond of Glasgow</u> on a voyage to Virginia for
tobacco. Robertson had sold the outward cargo and
spent most of the proceeds on a ship which he named
the <u>Albany</u>. He loaded it with tobacco and sailed to
Barbados and Jamaica. He is now in Inverness with the
ship, where he had sold the whole cargo.

AC9/818   **1723**

Archibald Yuill, shipmaster in Crawfordsdyke, owner of
the 120 ton <u>Jean</u> [formerly the <u>Brisbane</u>] master William
Pettigrew, v. Samuel McCaull and Company, merchants
in Glasgow, for freight of tobacco brought in his ship
from Virginia. Reference to Robert Dunlop in Virginia.

AC8/295   **1723**

Archibald Yuill, merchant in Glasgow, v. Wallace of
Camsifearn and others, freighters of his vessel to

Virginia. They owe 90 days demeurage at Virginia and have still not completely unloaded the ship.

AC9/862   1723

Henry Spencer and other members of the crew of the Queen Anne of Whitehaven, v. William Lewis, her master, for their wages due for a voyage from Virginia to Glasgow. Crew included Alexander Arbuthnott mate and supercargo, Richard Power, James Dinning, James Gillespie, and Richard Rymond.

AC9/868   1724

Thomas Walker, commander of the 160 ton Pearl of Whitehaven, v. Andrew Ramsay, merchant in Glasgow, concerning a voyage to Virginia for tobacco. Reference to William Noble chief mate of the Pearl, Solomon Paterson bosun of the Pearl, and William Hicks merchant in Whitehaven.

AC7/28/715-915; 33/44-204   July 26, 1723

Robert Bunteine of Airdoch and Thomas Fleming, merchant in Greenock, v. Walter Blair and Company, merchants in Glasgow, for payment of freight, demurrage and damage done on a voyage to Virginia and Maryland on the Cathcart of Greenock

AC7/28/1071-1097   **September 13, 1723**

Henry Spenser, James Gillespie, Richard Ryman, Richard Power and James Dunning, sailors of the <u>Queen Anne of Whitehaven</u> v. William Lowe, master, and Alexander Arbuthnott, merchant supercargo of the said ship, for non payment of wages due for a voyage for Boston, Massachusetts, to the River Potomac in Virginia and from there to Whitehaven.

AC7/28/1118-1135   **November 12, 1723**

Thomas Lutewidge, merchant in Whitehaven, and John Binning, writer in Edinburgh, his factor, v. William Lowes, master of the <u>Queen Anne</u>, James Thompson, carpenter in Dublin, and Robert Corson, ropemaker, owners of the said ship, for bringing back a cargo of damaged tobacco from Virginia too late for market.

AC7/28/1237-1261; 29/368-396, 456-553.
                                    December 6, 1723

Sale of the ship <u>Queen Anne of Whitehaven</u>. Thomas Lutewidge and John Binning v. William Lowe, James Thompson, Robert Crosver, Henry Spenser, James Gillespie, Richard Rydmer, Richard Power and James Dunning.

AC8/295   **1723**

Archibald Yuill, merchant of Glasgow, v. Wallace of
Camisfean and others, freighters of his ship to Virginia.
They owe 90 days demurrage at Virginia and have still
not completely unloaded the ship.

AC9/818   **1723**

Archibald Yuille, shipmaster of Crawfordyke, owner of
the 120 ton <u>Jean</u> formerly the <u>Brisbane</u>, master William
Pettigrew, skipper in Crawfordyke, v. Samuel McCaull,
merchant in Glasgow, for freight of tobacco brought in
his ship from Virginia. Reference to Robert Dunlop in
Virginia, John Wallace of Camscan, John Murdoch,
William Codbert, and the crew of the <u>Jean</u>.

AC9/862   **1723**

Henry Spencer and the crew of the <u>Queen Anne of
Whitehaven</u> v. William Lewis, her master, for their
wages for a voyage from Virginia to Glasgow.

AC8/310   **1725**

Thomas Coats, merchant in Whitehaven, and the other
owners of the <u>Mary and Frances of Whitehaven</u>,
commander John Hodgeson of Whitehaven, v. Robert
Robertson and Arthur Tran, merchants of Glasgow, for

demurrage arising from a voyage to Maryland or Virginia.

AC9/925   **1725**

William Fulton, carpenter on the <u>Diligence of Glasgow</u> and the other crew members, v. her master Captain John Hamilton for wages due for a voyage to the Potomac River, Virginia. Reference to Hugh Kennedy, a merchant in Glasgow and in Virginia, and the crew of the <u>Diligence</u> – mate David Spreull, bosun Robert Forbes, cook Christopher Wall, David Petrie, James Baillie, William Anderson, Thomas Ludat, Hugh Ferguson, and George Lyon.

AC7/31/1170-1212   **August 13, 1725**

The crew of the <u>Diligence of Glasgow</u> v. Captain John Hamilton, master of the said ship, for non payment of wages on the voyage to the Potomac and back.

AC7/31/1458-1644   **November 16, 1725**

Clement Nicolson, merchant, and others, owners of the <u>Kent of Whitehaven</u>, Joseph Gale, master of the said ship, and John Binning, writer in Edinburgh, their factor, v. Charles Miller, merchant and provost of Glasgow, and John Stirling, merchant and late baillie there, concerning a cargo of tobacco from Virginia.

AC9/966   **1726**

Clement Nicholson, a merchant in Whitehaven, and the owners of the <u>Kent of Whitehaven</u>, master Joseph Gale, v. Charles Millar, provost of Glasgow, re freight on a cargo of tobacco from Virginia. Reference to the <u>Amity of Whitehaven</u>, <u>Rappahannock of Whitehaven</u>, <u>Greenock of Glasgow</u>, <u>Adventure of Whitehaven,</u> and the <u>Globe of Whitehaven,</u> the crew of the <u>Kent</u> carpenter Thomas Millar, mate John Wilson, Samuel Hobart, John Peill, Thomas Smithson, John Smith, William Hellon, William Craine, Paul Parker and John Nicholson, plus various merchants in Glasgow and in Rotterdam.

AC9/6398   **1726**

Andrew and Neil Buchanan v. Robert Buntine of Ardoch, with whose late partner Thomas Fleming, merchant in Greenock, they had a charter party in 1723 for the <u>Cathcart of Greenock</u> for a voyage to Virginia for tobacco.

AC9/967   **1726**

Captain James McCulloch and Company in Belfast, owners of the <u>Mary</u> galley, James Baillie master, v. Robert Allan of Belfast, who chartered the ship for a voyage to Barbados, for demurrage because the ship exceeded her agreed time in Barbados by six months. The case is brought in Scotland because the ship is at Glasgow. Reference to Edward McCormack, mate of the

Mary, John Cunningham, merchant in Glasgow, Thomas
Wallace of Carnhill, merchant in Glasgow, Hugh
Ronalds, cooper in Port Glasgow, James Mears,
merchant in Belfast, James McCaver, carpenter on the
Mary, David Blair and John Clerk, shipmasters in Port
Glasgow.

AC7/32/116-213   January 28 and February 15, 1726

James McCulloch and Company of Belfast, owners of
the **Mary** galley, and James Mears, merchant there,
their factor, v. Robert Allan, a merchant in Belfast, for
demurrage and other damage incurred on a voyage
undertaken for the defender from Belfast to Barbados
and back to Glasgow, by being unduly detained in
Barbados by the defender.

AC9/976   1727

Edward Tubman, master of the **Mayflower of
Whitehaven** v. Michael and John Coulter, merchants in
Edinburgh, for freight for a voyage to Virginia for
tobacco.

AC9/1016   1727

Petition by William Fall and Brothers, merchants in
Dunbar, who had tobacco on the **James**, master James

Melville, which was damaged by a storm in the Moray Firth while returning from Virginia.

AC7/33/433-583   **July 14, 1727**

Robert Bogle jnr., Robert Robertson, John Gray, Arthur Tran, and Samuel McCaull, merchants in Glasgow, v. Alexander Horseburgh, supercargo and surgeon late of the <u>Hanover of Glasgow</u> a brigantine. Horseburgh had been commissioned in November 1719 to go from the Clyde to the coast of Guinea, thence to the West Indies and home to Port Glasgow, and to purchase with the outward cargo as many slaves as the said ship would stow, and with the rest of the cargo to purchase gold-dust, Elephants teeth, etc.

Horseburgh was charged with not accounting to the pursuers for all the slaves he purchased, as well as not reporting correctly the amounts of his sales.

At Guinea, Horseburgh shipped aboard the <u>Hanover</u> 135 negro slaves, men, women, boys and girls, whereof 87 living negro men, women, boys and girls were delivered from the said ship to Horsburgh in October and November 1720, viz. four at Barbados, three at Nevis, and the rest at Basseterre and Old Road in St Kitts.

Horseburgh in a letter to Thomas Thomson, a merchant in Glasgow, now deceased, partner to one of the pursuers, from Old Calabar, June 9, 1720, states that he has 90 slaves on board for which he has paid 70 or 75 coppers per head for men and 60 for women, which 18 pence per copper equals £5.5 shillings or £5 12

shillings and sixpence sterling for the men and £4 10 shillings for the women.

In a second letter to Thomson from Barbados dated November 1, 1720 Horseburgh advises him of his arrival there with only about 77 slaves, whereas in truth there were 80 remaining alive, two thirds of them having been purchased at Calabar. In a further letter from St Kitts dated November 26, 1720, Horseburgh states that he had disposed of all the slaves for near £24 per head round and that he was taking in sugar at 16 shillings per hundred sufficient to load the vessel.

AC9/1056   **1728**

Alexander Skene, brother of George Skene of that Ilk, v. John King, merchant in Glasgow, for money due after a voyage to Virginia as the supercargo of the Nightingale of Whitehaven with Claud Hamilton.

AC7/34/433-451   **April 26, 1728**
AC9/1056   **1728**

Alexander Skene, brother of George Skene of that Ilk, v. John King, Alexander Baillie, Walter Duncan, John Aitchison and John Bowman, merchants in Glasgow, who had sent him to Virginia in 1726 as a supercargo on the Nightingale of Whitehaven, and had omitted to pay his wages.

AC7/28/715-915; 33/44-204   July 26, 1728

Robert Buntine of Airdoch and Thomas Fleming, merchant in Greenock, v. Walter Blair and Company, merchants in Glasgow, for payment of freight, demurrage, and damage done on a voyage to Virginia and Maryland on the <u>Cathcart of Greenock</u>.

AC9/1042   1728

Alexander Horseburgh, surgeon in Glasgow, v. Robert Bogle jnr. and four other Glasgow merchants in connection with a slaving voyage made by the brigantine <u>Hanover of Glasgow</u>, master Garrett Garretts, in 1719. Horseburgh was the supercargo and is accused by his employers of mishandling transactions during the voyage. Reference to John Kerr, second mate on the <u>Hanover of Glasgow</u>, Robert Robertson, John Gray, Arthur Tran, and Samuel McCall, all merchants in Glasgow.

AC7/34/697-708   November 6, 1728

John Lyon, a merchant in Port Glasgow, v. John Hay, John Riddell, John Gray and John Buchanan, merchants in Glasgow. Lyon had hired his ship the <u>Nanino</u> for a voyage to South Carolina, and was suing for non-payment of freight charges.

AC7/34/708-740   **November 8, 1728**

Edward Lowis, master of the <u>Centurion of Whitehaven</u>, Elizabeth Lowis, and John Binning, factor, v. Henry McCaull, John McFarlane and Thomas Yuille, merchants in Glasgow, who had failed to pay freight on tobacco brought from Virginia.

AC10/132   **1728**

Petition by William Fraser and Thomas Alves baillies of Inverness, and George Dunbar, eldest son of late James Dunbar. In 1721 each of the petitioners purchased a one-sixteenth share in the <u>Joseph of Dundee</u> from her master Thomas Baillie, son of Hugh Baillie, former Sheriff Clerk of Ross. Baillie owes them for profits from 1721-1723 and for credit advanced to him and not repaid.

In 1723 the ship was wrecked on the Aberdeenshire coast, when going south from the Moray Firth. Baillie had insured her at Rotterdam for a sum greater that his share. He received the insurance money but did not inform the petitioners. After the loss of the <u>Joseph</u> the petitioners made Baillie master of another ship of theirs, which was also wrecked.

After the second wreck, they appointed Baillie master of another ship in which he had made many voyages to the Straits and elsewhere but has kept away from Scotland. He is now in Inverness loading for Virginia but refuses to account with the petitioners. He intends

to sail shortly and the petitioners ask that he be
arrested and settle what he owes them.

AC10/136   **1728**

**Petition by William Hunter, master of the <u>Hanover of
Irvine</u>. The <u>Hanover</u> was partly owned by John
Crichton, merchant in Irvine, debtor of John Boyd
master of the <u>John of Irvine</u>, who has had the <u>Hanover</u>
arrested. The ship was at Irvine freighted for Virginia.**

AC10/137   **1728**

**Petition by John King, Walter Dundas, Alexander Baillie,
John Hutchison and William Bowman, merchants in
Glasgow, who having heard that Alexander Skene is
going abroad ask that he be arrested. Alexander
Skene, brother of George Skene of that Ilk, had been
employed by them as a supercargo on a voyage to
Virginia on the <u>Nightingale of Whitehaven</u> in 1726 and
had sold the outward cargo on wholesale terms instead
of on retail terms thus causing financial loss to his
employers.**

AC10/138   **1728**

**Petition by John McFarlane, Charles Robertson and
Company, merchants in Glasgow, who had employed
William McKnight as a supercargo to go to Barbados on**

the snow <u>John and David of Port Glasgow</u> who had returned without providing an account of his transactions on behalf of his employers.

AC10/136   1728

Petition by William Hunter, master of the <u>Hanover of Irvine</u>. John Crichton, merchant in Irvine, owns one sixteenth of the <u>Hanover</u> but the ship has been arrested by his creditor John Boyd, master of the said ship. The ship is lying at Irvine freighted for Virginia. As was usual in such cases the Court allowed to ship to sail provided the skipper guaranteed to return to his port of departure.

AC10/151   1729

Petition by baillie William McKay and Company, William Fraser and Thomas Alves, merchants in Inverness, v. David Tolmie, master of the <u>Mary of Inverness</u> and his mate David Robertson, son of John Robertson of Lyne. The ship had been freighted for a voyage to Virginia for tobacco but on her return Tolmie and Robertson sold most of the tobacco in Ireland.

AC10/152   1729

Petition by William Fall and Company, merchants in Dunbar. The petitioners had imported tobacco from Virginia to Dunbar which had been sold by Alexander

Lindsay, merchant in Duns, Berwickshire, without their permission. As he intends to move to Northumberland the petitioners request that he be arrested.

AC9/1070   **1729**

Edward Lows, master of the <u>Centurion of Whitehaven</u>, v. John MacFarlane and Company in Glasgow, concerning two voyages to Virginia. Reference to Henry McCall, merchant in Glasgow, Clement Nicholson, merchant in Whitehaven, Thomas Yuill, merchant in Glasgow, George Bogle, merchant in Glasgow, and John Hamilton, merchant in Whitehaven.

AC9/1085   **1729**

George Currie and George Thomson, merchants in Glasgow, v. Neil Buchan, merchant in Glasgow, and other insurers of the <u>Fortune of Glasgow</u>, master James Porter, which was lost returning from Virginia with tobacco. Reference to Andrew Ramsay, Andrew Cochrane, James Spreull, John Luke jnr., and William Anderson, all merchants, and John Woodrow MD.

AC9/1116   **1730**

Thomas Lutewidge, merchant of Whitehaven, owner of the <u>Wharton of Whitehaven</u>, master James Wharrey, v. Archibald Gray and Company, merchants in Glasgow, concerning tobacco imported from Virginia on his ship

in 1724-1725. Reference to Walter Corbett, John Buchanan, John King, and John Dunlop, all merchants in Glasgow, and Thomas Knight, mayor of Youghall, Ireland, and Bernard Smith, pilot in Youghall.
AC7/35/58-200   January 13, 1730

Thomas Lutwidge in Whitehaven v Archibald Gray, John Buchanan and John King, merchants in Glasgow, who had hired his ship the <u>Wharton</u> to bring tobacco from Virginia. The ship was wrecked on the return voyage but the cargo was saved. Lutwidge desires payment of freight

AC9/1098   1730

John Blair, merchant in Glasgow, v. William Cunningham and three other Glasgow merchants, his former employers, for expenses as supercargo on the brigantine <u>Lillie of Glasgow</u> in 1726. The said ship had sailed to the West Indies, when Britain was at war with Spain, it joined a convoy from Jamaica escorted by <u>HMS Leopard</u> on the return voyage. She was unable to keep up and was taken by a Havannah based privateer. Reference to Archibald Hyndman, master of the <u>Happy Return of Port Glasgow</u>, William Dunlop, master of the <u>America of Glasgow</u>, Thomas Walker, master of the <u>Pearl of Whitehaven</u>, and J. Kilpatrick, master of the <u>Favour of Whitehaven</u>.

AC9/1104   **1730**

Adam Boyd and James Hall, merchants in Greenock, owners of the <u>Jean of Greenock</u>, late master John Easdale deceased, v. John Stark and Company, proprietors of the Wester Sugar House of Glasgow, for breach of a charter party in a voyage to Jamaica for sugar during which Easdale died. Reference to James Graham, supercargo on the said voyage, William Warden, mariner on the <u>Jean</u>, William Craig, William Anderson, and Robert Clark, merchants in Glasgow, and James Boyd, merchant in Greenock.

AC7/35/354-364   **March 3, 1730**

The crew of the <u>Betty of Glasgow</u> a doggar v. Andrew and Archibald Gray, merchants in Glasgow, for wages due on a voyage from Port Glasgow to Jamaica and return.

AC7/35/485-529   **April 21, 1730**

John Blane, merchant in Glasgow, v. William Cunningham, John Baird, Thomas Wallace, and Matthew Crawford, merchants in Glasgow. Blane had gone to Jamaica as supercargo on the brigantine <u>Lillie</u>, he had been taken by Spanish privateers on the return voyage and had various adventures. He wanted his wages and expenses of passage home.

AC7/35/1065-1134   **November 27, 1730**

Adam Boyd and James Hall, merchants in Greenock, owners of the <u>Jean</u>, v. John Stark, William Anderson and William Craig, merchants in Glasgow, for freight and demurrage due on a voyage from Greenock to Jamaica and back.

AC7/36/17-28   **January 15, 1731**

John White, Samuel Worsley, George Tod, James Gregory, John Taylor, sailors, Walter Montgomerie, carpenter, on the <u>Cathcart of Glasgow</u>, and their factor James Crawford v. Robert Rae, shipmaster in Greenock, for wages due for a voyage from the Clyde to Quantico on the Potomac River, taking 8 months and 10 days from February 8 to October 15, 1724.

AC7/36/328-338   **March 12, 1731**

James Gibson, a merchant, late in Glasgow, now of Pungataigue Creek, Accomack County, Virginia, v. James Blair, John Gray, Robert McGowan, merchants in Glasgow, and John Armour, tailor and late deacon convenor of the trades there, and Samuel Taylor, for money owing as partner and freighter in a cargo sent from Port Glasgow to Virginia on the <u>Brisbane of Port Glasgow</u> to Virginia and Maryland in 1727

AC7/36/506-512   **May 7, 1731**

Hugh Vans, merchant in Boston, New England, and his factor John Starke, a merchant in Glasgow, v. Archibald Yuill, shipmaster and merchant in Port Glasgow, and James Hamilton, shipmaster there, re the sale of the ship <u>Brisbane</u>.

AC9/1159   **1731**

William Clogess and Elisha Bidles, mariners in Philadelphia, v. John Symms, master of the brigantine <u>Mary of Philadelphia</u> for wages due for a voyage from Philadelphia via Virginia to Dunbar. The ship is now freighted for a voyage to Lisbon and the pursuers want an undertaing that she will return to Philadelphia. Reference to the crew of the <u>Mary</u> including Hugh McRennett, Thomas Needs, and Joseph Topps.

AC7/37   **November 7, 1732**

William Porter and John Niven, sailors in Ayr, and their factor Zacharias Gemmill, v. William Reid, shipmaster in Ayr, for wages due on a voyage from April 9, 1730 to October 6, 1731 from the Clyde via Hamburg, Cork, Madeira, Barbados, Virginia, back to Madeira, Barbados, Antigua, and back to Port Glasgow.

AC9/1196   **1732**

Hugh Vans, merchant in Boston, New England, and his factor John Stark a merchant in Glasgow, v. Archibald Yuille, a merchant in Port Glasgow, for payment of bottomry on his ship the 140 ton <u>Brisbane of Port Glasgow</u>, skipper James Hamilton. Reference to John Clerk, shipmaster, Robert Gilmour in Crawfordsdyke, and Samuel Welch merchant in Edinburgh.

AC9/1248   **1733**

Robert Scott, mate, and other crew of the <u>William and John of Glasgow</u>, pursue tow of her owners, Thomas Calder, a merchant, and John Robertson, a writer in Glasgow, for their wages for a voyage to Virginia. Reference to the crew of the <u>William and John</u>, John Sangster carpenter, Duncan McCaustelin bo'sun, John Kinloch cooper, Alexander Crighton cook, Matthew Murphy mariner, Daniel McKay mariner, John Haliway mariner, and Thomas Craimare mariner, also to James Corbett jnr. A merchant in Glasgow, and to Archibald Murchie a shipmaster in Crawforddykes.

AC7/40/166-243   **February 22 & April 23, 1734**

Robert Auld, master of the <u>Pelican of Saltcoats</u>, v. James Montier, later master of the said ship, Peter Montgomery, William Gordon, and Henry McCaull, all merchants in Glasgow, for freight and demurrage due for unnecessarily detaining the ship on a voyage from

Saltcoats to Cork, Barbados, Antigua, Tarbet, Loch Ryan, and Port Glasgow.

AC7/40/86-115   **April 9. 1734**

Hugh Vans in Boston, New England, and John Starke, merchant in Glasgow, his factor v. Archibald Yuill and James Hamilton, shipmasters and merchants in Glasgow, re sale of the ship <u>Brisbane</u>.

AC7/40/137-142   **April 16, 1734**
AC8/498   **1734**

Archibald Gray and John King, merchants in Glasgow, v. John Buchanan, merchant in Glasgow, a dispute over payment for the freight of the <u>Wharton of Whitehaven</u> , master James Whary, for a voyage to Virginia in 1725.

AC7/40/276-285   **June 7, 1734**

William Mackay jnr., Duff Mackay and Company, merchants in Inverness v. Andrew Munro, merchant in Inverness and Daniel Mackay, merchant in London, for £2000 sterling, with interest, as the value of two loadings of goods imported in two of their ships, the <u>Lark</u> and the <u>Swallow</u>.

AC9/1301   1734

Matthew Robertson, formerly a shipmaster in Bo'ness, then resident in Edinburgh, v. William Dundas, merchant in Rotterdam. Dundas owed John Laing, formerly a merchant in Cromarty, then a Minister of the Gospel in Maryland, for fish exported by him from Cromarty to Bilboa in Robertson's ship the <u>Hope of Bo'ness</u>.

AC9/1297   1734

Hugh Vans, merchant in Boston, New England, and his factor John Stark provost of Glasgow, v. Captain Archibald Yuille, merchant in Port Glasgow. For payment of a bill of bottomry on his ship the <u>Brisbane</u>, granted at Boston by her master James Hamilton, shipmaster of Port Glasgow.

AC10/194   1734

Petition by William Boyle, shipmaster in Bo'ness, master of the <u>Marjory</u>. Boyle had hired Alexander Boyd, mariner of Glasgow as first mate, John Addison, mariner of Bo'ness as second mate, and Andrew Walk mariner of Bo'ness as cook to serve on a voyage to Jamaica under charter to Samuel Weston, baillie of Edinburgh. The three men had deserted and Boyle applied for a warrant for their arrest and imprisonment until they find a guarantor that they will undertake the voyage.

AC9/1354   **1736**

McReadie v. Baillie and others. Hugh Baillie of Monkton advocate, pursues james Montier former master of the **Prosperity of Glasgow** of which Montier is part owner. In 1732 Baillie had goods aboard the **Prosperity** which were to be sold in Virginia by Montier who then had to buy tobacco and barrel staves with the proceeds.

Reference to the crew of the **Prosperity**, Abraham Hasty mate, Robert Aitken carpenter, Archibald Taylor, David Longhead, and John Swordy, also to Hugh McBride of Badlan, James Ferguson writer in Ayr, Alexander Baillie merchant in Kilwinning, and others.

AC10/246   **1736**
AC13/1   **April 28, 1737**

Charter party between Robert Bryson, shipmaster in Leith, master of the **Ann of Edinburgh**, and Gustavus Sinclair, Samuel Welsh, and Archibald Balfour, merchants in Edinburgh, for a voyage from Leith to Boston, New England, and back.

Stipulations:
(1) As Bryson is unable to go on the voyage, James Blair will navigate the ship on the outward leg and until the cargo is loaded.

(2) **Patrick Houstoun is to be employed as mate on the outward voyage, and is to take over as master of the ship on the return voyage.**

(3) **The freighters will maintain any passengers or servants which they put onto the ship**

(4) **The freighters will employ a carpenter to grave and caulk the ship from the bends downwards, before she leaves Leith.**

AC8/541   **1737**

John Brauchill v. James Scott. John Brauchill, a mariner, was hired by James Scott, master of the <u>America</u> for a voyage from the Clyde to Virginia. Brauchill claims to have been attacked by Scott and put ashore on the coast of Virginia.

AC7/43/4-213   **January 6, 1738**
AC9/1425   **1738**

William Bryce, a merchant in Glasgow, v. Ninian Bryce, a shipmaster in Glasgow. In March 1731 the pursuer had entrusted seven casks of Wood's hall-pence to the defender in his voyage from the Clyde to New England on the <u>Betty</u> doggar, master John Somerville, also cutlery; he had expected tobacco in return.

Reference to Hugh Vans merchant in Boston, James
Calhoun merchant in Edinburgh, Arthur Tran, Peter
Murdoch, Laurence Colquhoun Hugh Rodger, John
Baird, John King, Thomas Clark, James Anderson, and
James Crawford all merchants in Glasgow; Zachariah
Stone and William Tuck in Boston; James Crockett,
John Crockett, George Seaman, John Hay, John Rigg
and George Ronald, merchants in Charleston, South
Carolina.

AC7/43/493-560   January 31 & June 27, 1738
AC9/1417   1738

James Hunter, tobacconist, William Blyth, tailor, and
Robert Brysson, shipmaster, all of Leith, v. Gustavus
Sinclair, Samuel Welsh, and Archibald Balfour,
merchants in Edinburgh, re payment of the ship <u>Ann of
Edinburgh</u>, for a voyage from Leith to Boston or any
other port in North America and back. The ship ran
aground on the coast near Boston and was sold by the
master without consulting the owners.

Reference to Alexander Middleton a merchant in
Boston, Robert Bryson shoemaster in Leith late master
of the <u>Ann</u>, David Banks his mate, Alexander Thomson
master of the <u>John of London</u>, George Mathison his
mate formerly second mate on the <u>Cumberland</u>, George
Moncreiff master of the brig <u>Alexander</u>, Captain
Archibald Edmonstone, John Bowman his mate, etc.

AC7/43/213-353   **February 14, 1738**

Executors of Andrew Ross v. Charles Crockatt, merchant in Edinburgh, James and John Crockatt, merchants in Charleston, South Carolina, James Seaman and John Crockatt jnr., also in Charleston, suing for the recovery of goods, gear and effects shipped to South Carolina.

AC7/44/287-296   **March 9, 1738**
AC8/599

Alexander Davidson, a bookseller in Inverness, lately in Edinburgh, v. William Backshell, a merchant in London, and Captain Joseph Avery, who had entered into a contract to transport people to South Carolina 'to plant a Landgravate and a Lordship', said to be the property of Joseph Avery, but had failed to transport the said Alexander Davidson and family, although he had paid the £13 passage money. The contract had been with Peter McCathie, a merchant in London and owner of the brigantine Hope, Captain Urquhart, which was sent to Leith to embark servants and others. Kenneth McKenzie of Blackwater, Avery's brother in law, made arrangements with Davidson in November 1736 to take him, his wife, child and a servant Jean Inch to South

Carolina for £13 sterling. Davidson put his goods and personal items aboard the ship at Leith on 2 December 1736 and was told by Daniel Bell, the supercargo, that he would be advised when the ship was to sail. However the ship sailed without the Davidsons who followed it to Cromarty. Alexander Davidson then applied to the Sheriff of Inverness for the arrest of Avery and the ship. Reference to George McKenzie, merchant in Cromarty, John Stewart, baillie of Inverness, and John McLean, merchant in London.

AC744/185-238; 268-286   January 23, 1739

Alexander Thomson, shipmaster in Leith, and William Nicoll, merchant in Edinburgh, his factor, v. Alexander Dundas and John Thomson, merchants in London, Jonathan Clerk and John Gutteridge, merchants in Boston, Archibald Cockburn and James Watson, merchants in Edinburgh, re the <u>John of Portsmouth, New Hampshire</u>, a brigantine, and a cargo of timber purchased in Boston and brought to Leith.

AC7/44/488-563   July 13, 1739

Richard and Alexander Oswald, merchants in Glasgow, v. William and Henry Hogg and David Young, merchants in Glasgow, and James Weir, commander of the <u>Diamond of Glasgow</u>, concerning a cargo of tobacco shipped on board the said ship in the River Potomac on September 22, 1738. The <u>Diamond</u> instead of coming as directly as possible to Glasgow or Greenock put off time at Fort William or elsewhere.

AC9/1443   **1739**

Alexander Oswald and Company, merchants in Glasgow, v. William and Henry Foggo and David Young, merchants in Glasgow and owners of the <u>Diamond of Glasgow</u>, master James Weir. Oswald and Company had tobacco on the <u>Diamond</u> which instead of returning directly to Greenock as per charter party the ship was directed by its owners to the Western Isles.

Reference to John Harvie in Virginia, George Turberville in Virginia, William Craig, John Bogle, John Baird, John Jamieson, Archibald Buchanan, John Gartshore, and Andrew Cathcart, all merchants in Glasgow, and Robert Arthur, shipmaster in Crawforddyke.

AC7/45/666-743   **July 25, 1740**

Matthew Robertson, shipmaster in Bo'ness, v. Archibald Hamilton, merchant in Edinburgh, and Mr Hugh Hamilton, chamberlain to the Duke of Hamilton. The pursuer had entered into an agreement with John Laing, merchant in Cromarty, later in Maryland, to freight a vessel for Hamburg or any port in Norway.

AC10/279   **1740**

Petition by George Forbes jnr., merchant in Aberdeen, for a warrant to search the ...., Captain Alexander Jamieson, now in Leith Roads bound for the West Indies, for William Petrie, a former merchant in Huntly, Aberdeenshire, debtor to the petitioner.

AC9/1472   **1741**

John Lumsden jnr., shipmaster in Aberdeen, part-owner and master of the <u>Theodosia of Aberdeen</u>, v. John Burnett, merchant in Aberdeen, and the other owners of the ship. The <u>Theodosia</u>, formerly the <u>Guernsey Lilly of London</u>, was a square sterned ship, about 50 tons, which had been built in Boston in 1733. It had been freighted for a voyage to Danzig but had gone ashore on a Swedish sandbank.

AC9/1476   **1741**

Hugh Cathcart, merchant in Glasgow, v. John Coulter, merchant in Glasgow. Hugh Cathcart, merchant in Glasgow and brother of the late Andrew Cathcart, merchant there, requested the suspension of the auction of the 300 ton <u>Baltimore of Glasgow</u>. Andrew Cathcart had been a member of a partnership formed in 1739 to have the ship built in New England [carpenters and materials being sent there for the purpose] and establish a storehouse in Maryland to be overseen by William Graham. The ship made one successful voyage and the partners now want to sell her, whereas Cathcart wants her to make a second voyage. The process contains many details of the operation, including a number of letters from the partners to James Graham. Reference to John Coulter, Andrew Aiton, Joh Luke, and Lawrence Dinwiddie, all merchants in Glasgow.

AC9/1514   1741

Elizabeth Cumberledge of Fulham, widow of Christopher Cumberledge, and her factor John Hamilton, Writer to the Signet, v. William Jones of Middlesex, commander of the 80 ton snow or sloop St David of London which had been built in Boston, New England.

AC9/1483   1742

John Baird, James Aitkin, William Alexander, John Cameron, and James Millar, mariners in Irvine, v. John Aitken, master of the Friendship of Ayr, for wages due for a voyage to Virginia. The skipper claims that the crew performed mutinous acts.

AC9/1487   1742

William Jones, master of the snow St David of London or of Dysart v. his mate Edward Jones, now of Leith, concerning a voyage to Philadelphia. Reference to James Watt, brewer in Leith, Robert Bull, a merchant in Leith, and George Ritchie, a cooper in Leith.

AC8/650 **1744**

Humphrey Stock, mate, and other crew of the <u>Charming Rachel of London</u> v. John Perkins, her master, for their wages for a voyage from London to Carolina and back to Leith.

Reference to the crew of the <u>Charming Rachel</u> – William Millar bo'sun, Bernard White, William Maddocks, William Pain, James Berry, Tim McKay, John Baptista snr. and John Baptista jnr.

AC9/1605 **1744**

Patrick Urquhart, merchant in Fraserburgh, Aberdeenshire, v. Peter McHattie, merchant in London, who employed the late George Urquhart, shipmaster in Fraserburgh, [brother german to Patrick Urquhart] as amster of his ship the <u>Hope</u> for a voyage to Carolina. George fell ill on the homeward voyage and died at the house of McHattie, who intromitted with his effects and also various expenses of he voyage.

Reference to James Bartlett, merchant in Banff.

AC8/659 **1745**

Peter Barclay, merchant in Virginia, at present in Edinburgh, v. David Young, master of the snow <u>Joseph and Ann</u>, for whom he paid various charges in Virginia.

Young drew bills for payment on William Bodwin and Andrew Daniel, merchants in London.

AC10/317   **1746**

Petition by William Wilson, commander of the <u>Hannah of Rotterdam</u>, for the arrest of Adam Apler, a coachmaker from Wurtemberg, (then in Edinburgh), and for Apler's factor, an Edinburgh periwigmaker named John Cruso. Apler and Cruso had caused Wilson to be imprisoned in Edinburgh Tolbooth on charges subsequently found to be baseless – charges concerning a contract with Apler and other Palatine passengers for passage to Philadelphia. Consequently Wilson sought Apler's arrest and a court order for Apler to pay Wilson's legalexpenses. Robert Cormack, acting for Apler, reported that the latter was "on board this day, and sails tomorrow".

AC10/318   **1746**

Petition by George Adam Apler, coachmaker of Wurtemburg, for the arrest of William Wilson and of George Laudenberg, stocking-weaver in Ebing, Wurtemburg. Apler, with his wife and three children, had taken passage with Wilson to Philadelphia which he had paid for in advance. His wife and two of his children had died on the voyage from Rotterdam to Leith and the other child had died since the ship had arrived in Scotland. Apler had decided not to continue with the voyage but Captain Wilson will not hand over the locked chest which contains all of Apler's valuables and Laudenberg, another passenger on the ship, owes him money.

AC9/1626   1747

James Watt, merchant in Greenock, v. John Dalrymple, now Lieutenant of the Royal Scots Regiment but then an Ensign in one of the American regiments. In 1741 there was a military expedition to Carthagena. At the time Watt's ship the Roanoke, master James Hunter, was in North Carolina, was requisitioned to carry troops to Jamaica. There, Dalrymple seized her victualling, took some of the crew and had the mate imprisoned. The master had to grant a bottomry in order to reprovision, but died soon after and the ship was left as a wreck. Alexander MacFarlane, merchant in Kingston, Jamaica, who held the bottomry, had to sell her. [She was originally the Trial, a 67 ton gaff-rigged sloop, launched in 1738 and bought in Massachusetts for Watt by Hugh Vans of Boston.

AC8/689   1747

John Morrison jnr., merchant in Aberdeen, and other owners of the Bonaccord of Aberdeen, master William Ross, v. John Forbes of Badiefurrow for freight for a voyage from Aberdeen to Virginia and Maryland. On her return journey the ship was cast away on Barren Island in Chesapeake Bay. Reference to William McKenzie, John McKenzie, John Fraser and James Young, all merchants in Aberdeen, Andrew Dyce shipmaster in Aberdeen, his brother James Dyce of Disblair and his daughter Janet.

AC10/323   **1747**

Petition by James Flint, brewer and baillie in Edinburgh, for the arrest of Robert Cochran, furniture painter in Edinburgh, his debtor, whose goods are on the <u>Magdalene</u>, master James McKenzie, currently in Leith bound for Carolina.

AC9/6455   **1748**

Hugh Milliken and baillie John Lyon, merchants in Glasgow, v. Alexander Nisbet, merchant in Edinburgh, in connection with goods sent to him in 1731 when he was a factor in Charleston, South Carolina. Goods sent to Nisbet when in Charleston included cloth, sugar and claret on board the <u>Euphemia</u>, master James Lyon, in return he sent tar, pitch, turpentine and rice. Problem involved the rates of exchange between British and Carolinian currencies.

Reference to – James Glen, Governor of South Carolina, Abraham Croft notary public there, James Michie attorney there, plus Roger Moore, Samuel Bowman, Abraham Smith, John Fraser, John Dart, James Fowler,

Isaac Holmes, George Austin, William Yeomans, Benjamin Smith, and Othneil Beale, all merchants in Charleston; also to Richard Oswald and Alexander Oswald, merchants in Glasgow, Archibald Stewart Writer to the Signet, Francis Harsnep master of the <u>Providence of Liverpool</u>, John Brakell master of the <u>Hannah of Liverpool</u>, Thomas Worstenholme and Brian Blundell, merchants in Liverpool.

AC10/335-7   1748

Petition by James Watson, merchant in Greenock, factor to John Anderson baillie of Greenock, for the uplifting of a cargo of tobacco on board the <u>Annabella of Greenock</u>, shipped from Virginia by Robert Tod, merchant there. This tobacco which belonged to Anderson had been arrested by one of his creditors William Donaldson, merchant in Glasgow.

AC10/339   1748

Petition by Thomas Gardner, merchant in Edinburgh, and Robert Douglas, merchant in Leith, for the arrest of Hugh Douglas, son of the said Robert, who was contracted to sail on his ship the <u>James of Dundee</u>, for a voyage from Leith to Virginia, but had subsequently enlisted as a soldier by Lieutenant John Adair of Marjorybank's Regiment in the service of the States General of Holland and was by then aboard a transport ship in Leith Roads.

AC11/231   **1748**

Bond of Caution. Robert Donald and Robert Rae,
merchants, and John Alexander, writer in Greenock,
John Anderson, merchant in Greenock, and his factor
James Watson, merchant in Greenock to ensure that
the cargo of tobacco on board the <u>Annabella of
Saltcoats</u>, master Thomas Knox, belonging to Robert
Todd, a merchant in Virginia, will be forthcoming to
William Donaldson, merchant in Glasgow.

AC9/1708   **1749**

Wardrop v. Burnet. John Wardrop, writer, and James
Neilson, a merchant in Glasgow, and Hugh Milliken,
merchant of Port Glasgow, owners of the snow <u>St
Andrew of Glasgow</u>, they pursue John Burnet, a
merchant in Aberdeen, for freight of tobacco from the
River Sarafras, Maryland, to the east coast of Scotland.

AC9/6464   **1749**

John Burnett, merchant in Aberdeen, v. John
Auchenleck, mariner in Dundee, who he engaged as
master of his snow the <u>Elizabeth of London</u> for a voyage
to Maryland in 1744. The ship was storm-damaged on
the voyage home and put into Stromness in the
Orkneys, where she stayed for a long time increasing
the damage already caused to her cargo of tobacco.

AC9/1658 1749

William Donaldson, merchant in Glasgow, attorney for
Henry Foggo, merchant in Glasgow, v. Robert Tod,
merchant in Norfolk, Virginia, for payment of goods
shipped to him on the Friendship in 1744. The cargo of
tobacco has been arrested in the hands of Thomas
Knox, master of the Annabella, and John Anderson,
merchant in Glasgow. Reference to James Whitelaw
and David Henry, saddlers, and to Andrew Ayton, Robert
Finlayson, John Dougal, Robert Scott jnr., Richard Bell,
and Archibald Campbell, all merchants in Glasgow.

AC9/1866/109 June 8, 1749

John and Alexander Harvey in Barbados v. Archibald
and John Coats, merchants in Glasgow.

AC8/723 1749

Captain Hugh Clerk, merchant in Edinburgh, v. James
Duncanson, shipwright in Airth, Stirlingshire. In 1748
Clerk fitted out the Industry for a voyage to Carolina.
Her master Andrew Cowan jnr., hired Duncanson as a
ships carpenter but he failed to join the ship and Clerk
was obliged to hire a young man, far from being expert
and well skilled in his business.

AC9/1748   **1750**

James Dyce and others, owners of the 100 ton
<u>Diligence of Aberdeen</u>, master George Duncan,
shipmaster in Aberdeen, v. William Copland and
Company, merchants in Aberdeen, for freight for a
voyage from Aberdeen to Maryland.

AC12/1712   **1750**

Robert Rae, merchant in Greenock, v. Robert Buntine of
Ardoch and others, for his wages as master of the
<u>Cathcart</u> to Maryland and Virginia in 1724. Reference to
the crew – Walter Montgomery carpenter, Alexander
Morrison bo'sun, Thomas Rae mate, Samuel Horsely
mariner, John Clerk boy, John Taylor boy, James
Gregory, John White, James Ross, George Todd, and
James Crawford.

AC9/1764   **1750**

Matthew Bogle, merchant in Glasgow, v. Thomas
Mitchell, former mate of the <u>President</u>. The ship had
been built in Boston, New England, the master was
Thomas Bogle and the supercargo was Robert Gilchrist.
On the voyage home Mitchell mutinied and
subsequently deserted.

AC9/1745 1750

Captain William Wilson, master of the <u>Anne Galley</u>, v. George Keppie, carpenter in Fisherrow, who was hired for a voyage from Leith to Carolina. Keppie deserted just before the ship set sail and she had to make the voyage without a carpenter, thus putting her in danger.

Reference to - Robert Cormack merchant in Leith, John Stewart shipmaster in Leith, Oliver Scott shoemaker in Fisherrow and Katherine Annand his wife, and Alexander Skirving merchant in Leith.

AC9/1746 1750

Thomas Mitchell, mariner in Irvine, former mate of the <u>President of Glasgow</u>, v. Matthew Bogle, merchant in Glasgow and owner of the ship, for his wages for a voyage to Virginia.

Reference to Thomas Bogle, shipmaster in Glasgow, John Cross, merchant in Glasgow, and Robert Gilchrist, merchant once in Glasgow then in Virginia.

AC10/283 1750

Petition for the arrest of George Moncrieff, who built a vessel in Boston, New England, in 1738. It was to have been about 120 tons and cost no more than £450 but turned out to be far larger and cost far more. Moncreiff named the ship the <u>Caledonia</u>. He then drew over £900 from Stewart and Ferguson in London to pay for the building, equipping, manning and stocking the first cargo and failed to account with the backers.

AC16/3/1-82   **November 4, 1751**

Samuel Lampo found guilty and sentenced to be transported to the American Plantations for life.

Samuel Lampo, shipmaster, a native of Yorkshire, commander of the ship <u>Prince Charles of Lorraine</u>, indicted before the High Court of the Admiralty and found guilty of willfully sinking the said ship off the coast of Cumberland in the month of May 1751 and having previously thereby predoniously disposed of part of the cargo in Cork and the rest in the Isle of Man stood in the pillory for the space of an hour with a label on his breast denoting his crime and a halter about his neck denoting his deserts. He was pelted by the populace with eggs and oranges. It is said that he would have suffered a more severe punishment had he law which makes his crime a felony reached this part of the United Kingdom and for which application has been made to Parliament.

The label stated "Here stands Samuel Lampo, an infamous person who died willfully and wickedly cast away the ship the <u>Prince Charles of Lorraine</u> with a design to defraud the users of the said ship after having, contrary to the trust reposed in him, sold the cargo aboard the said ship belonging to the merchants who had loaded the same" and after he was imprisoned until 19 November after which he was to be transported to HM Plantations in America at the first opportunity, and banished from Scotland for life – if he returned he was to be imprisoned for a year then whipped through the city on the first market day of each month, and then again transported.

AC16/2/277-407   **November 18, 1751**

James McNair, a Glasgow shipmaster and ship-owner, imprisoned in Edinburgh Tolbooth, son of Robert McNair a merchant in Glasgow, v. John Graham of Dugaldston , accused of over-insuring the brigantine <u>Jean</u> and its cargo for a voyage from Virginia to Barbados in 1750. The ship sailed from Virginia with James McNair as master and instead of taking the usual route he sailed via the coast of Bermuda where he scuttled it.

AC7/46/51-62   **June 25, August 21, 1754**

Richard Hartley, master of the snow <u>St George of Montrose</u> v. Thomas Douglas, John Addison, Robert Dunbar, James Smith jnr., Robert Dickie and Thomas Christie jnr., merchants in Montrose, suing for wages due to him for a voyage from Scotland to the coast of Africa, thence to the West Indies and back to Montrose.

"There was loaden aboard the said ship belonging to the said Thomas Douglas and Company upon the coast of Guinea at the date of the aforesaid assignation, or thereafter, three hundred negroes or slaves, which were carried to the Island of Antigua, or some other Island or Islands in the West Indies. And there the said Richard Hartley sold and disposed of them, at thirty pounds Sterling each amounting to the price of the whole to nine thousand pounds sterling."

AC7/46/101-106   July 5, 1754

Walter Orroch, merchant in Methil, v. Alexander Gordon, merchant in Boston, New England. The defender when in Scotland entered into an agreement with the pursuer, that a ship was to be sent from Scotland with a cargo of goods for the Boston market, the proceeds was to be used to build a ship there and freight it back with flax-seed for Scotland. This agreement was not held to.

AC7/46/212-233   August 23, 1754

John Freeman jnr., Thomas and Samuel Smith, merchant in Bristol, partners, and their factor Andrew Stewart, writer in Edinburgh, v. John Rowand, jnr., merchant in Glasgow, for £314 11 shillings owed for linen and other goods shipped aboard the Lamb, master John Price, for Carolina in 1753.

AC7/46/185-211   **August 30, 1754**

Henry Wauchope, a merchant late in Maryland, v. John Rowand, James Denniston and Robert Barry, merchants in Glasgow. The pursuer was employed by one of the said merchants, John Rowand, to take charge of a store in Virginia to receive cargoes from Glasgow, dispose of them, and with the proceeds send back to Glasgow cargoes of tobacco. In suing for a balance of five hundred pounds sterling, which he declares due to him for goods furnished to the aforesaid store.

AC7/47/598-602   **March 4, 1755**

John Trotter, merchant in Kingston, Jamaica, Walter Tullideph, late of Antigua, his attorney, James Dewar of Vogrie, and Robert Menzies, Writer to the Signet, v. Hugh McLauchlan snr., formerly a merchant in Leith, but now of Kingston, Jamaica.

McLauchlan and his family went from Leith to Jamaica on the snow <u>Adventure</u>, Captain James Hamilton. By previous agreement on his arrival in Jamaica he was to put on board the said ship 50 hogsheads of sugar and rum. However he only put on board nine, whence this action arose.

AC9/1960   **November 18, 1755**

John Carmichael, merchant in Edinburgh, v. George Seaman, merchant in South Carolina.

Carmichael had sent a consignment of goods [claret, sherry, enamelled china trenchers, sewing silk, linen, a set of weights and brass scales] worth £139 13 shillings 10 pence sterling to George Seaman in Charleston, South Carolina, on board the <u>Helen</u>, master James Seaman, in 1734 and had not been paid. Evidence includes a letter from George Seaman to John Deas.

AC7/47/32-597   **March 19, December 24, 1755**

James Coulter, James Spreull, Archibald Ingram, James Johnstone, John Cross, George Buchanan jnr., and George Anderson, merchants in Glasgow, v. Robert McNair and his son James McNair, merchants in Glasgow, regarding a policy of insurance for the ship <u>Jean,</u> master James McNair, and the goods therein, on a voyage from Virginia to Barbados.

AC7/48/970-973   **February 13, 1756**

James Mansfield, Sons, and Hunter, merchants in Edinburgh, v. John Elphinston, merchant in Aberdeen, for the value of goods sent to Antigua and Jamaica.

AC7/48/595-642　　　　　**March 30, April 13, 1756**

William Wemyss, writer in Edinburgh, v. Thomas Murray, master of the <u>Walmington</u>. James Stewart at St Thomas, Jamaica, put on board the said ship for the pursuer one puncheon of rum. Murray entered it as only 80 gallons at the Leith Customs House, and action is brought for the value of the difference between these two amounts.

AC7/48/930-933　　　　　**October 29, 1756**

John Adams, merchant and mason in Glasgow, v. William MacFarlane, sailor on the man-of-war <u>St George</u> for £5 1s 6p sterling, with interest, the value of 19.5 yards of broad muslin which he sold for the pursuer in Jamaica.

AC7/49/14-53　　　　　**December 21, 1756**

John Carmichael, merchant in Edinburgh, v. George Seaman, merchant in South Carolina, for £139 13s 10p sterling, with interest, for goods furnished.

AC7/49/1293-1534　　　　**October 7, November 11, 1757**

Alexander McDougall, auditor's clerk in the Exchequer, v. Robert Bailey and John McKenna, merchants in

Edinburgh, and Walter Scott, shipmaster of the **Elizabeth and Peggy of Leith** for money due on a shipment of goods to Carolina.

AC7/50   **July 8, October 3, 1760**

Claud Alexander of Newton v. James Johnston and John Wood, late merchants in Glasgow now in Virginia, for money due on a shipment of goods sent to the James River, Virginia, on the **Joanna of Glasgow**.

AC7/50   **April 7, July 28, and October 20, 1761**

William Tait, late carpenter on the **Molly of Glasgow**, for himself and as an attorney or trustee for other members of the crew of the said ship v. Captain John Douglas, commander of the **Molly**, Colin Dunlop and Andrew Buchanan, merchants in Glasgow, and James and George Buchanan, merchants in Glasgow, sons of Andrew Buchanan, for wages due on a voyage from Leith to St Kitts and for their share of a French ship captured on the return voyage.

Among the evidence offered in this trial was the following letter from Captain John Douglas to Adam Fairholm, banker in Edinburgh, and Duncan Pollock, shipmaster in Leith, dated September 19, 1757 –

"I take this opportunity of a ship for Amsterdam informing you of our good luck of taking a snow from Martinique to Bordeaux, laden with coffee, cotton and sugar, which I hope will be arrived with you before this gets to you. She's about one hundred and forty tons, no guns, three gentlemen passengers, and thirteen crew belonging to her, she is a New England built vessel, very well found in rigging and sails. Her hull looks to be newly repaired. The above snow had just taken a Virginia sloop, on our appearing she left her, after having made the said sloop come on board with their boat. Gave chase to the snow the fourteenth instant, made her good .."

AC7/50   **May 11, 1762**

Robert Tod, William Tod jnr., and Alexander Hepburn, merchants in Edinburgh, John Tod, carpenter in Leith, Richard Tod, merchant in Leith, trustees of Oliver Tod, merchant in Edinburgh, v. Charles Tod, sometime merchant in Kingston, Jamaica, now Captain in the service of the East India Company, and Archibald Tod of Hayfield, for money due on goods consigned by Oliver Tod, deceased, to John and Charles Tod, merchants in Kingston, Jamaica.

AC16/3/339-347   **July 13, 1765**

Peter Black, found guilty of assaulting Revenue Officers. He petitioned to be transported to America, which was granted for 14 years.

AC7/50   **December 6, 1763**

The British Linen Company and George Goldie, their present manager, v. William Hunter, pewterer in Edinburgh, and his wife, Alexander Ritchie, merchant in Edinburgh, and his wife, Jean Russell, mantua maker in Edinburgh, James and William Herriot, son of the deceased James Heriot in Edinburgh. Action brought against the defenders as executors of the estate of Dr William Horseburgh, of New Providence, deceased, at whose order six trunks of linen were shipped to him on board the <u>Sequiries</u> via South Carolina, and who died before payment was made.

AC7/51   **June 28, 1765**

William Gilchrist jnr., merchant in Kilmarnock, and John Glen of Auchincloss, Ayrshire, v. James Dunlop, merchant in Glasgow.

John Glen assigned to William Gilchrist his interest in six hogsheads of tobacco sent by Gardner Fleming, merchant in Virginia, on board the <u>Agnes</u> and consigned to Dunlop. Dunlop sold the tobacco, but did not make the necessary payment resulting therefrom to Gilchrist. The action is raised to recover payment.

AC7/51   **July 19, July 26, 1765**

Peter Paterson, writer in Glasgow, v. John Tennant, merchant in St Kitts.

William Cunningham made over to John Paterson, who in turn made over to Peter Paterson, a note of hand of James Ogilvie in St Croix for £329 6 shillings 1 pence. John Tennant collected payment on the note and paid part of it to Peter Paterson, who now brings action for the balance.

AC7/51   **July 26, 1765**

Alexander House, late one of the crew of the <u>Sally</u>, and Thomas Dallas, surgeon in Musselburgh, appointed by the judge as his curator, v. David Loch, merchant in Leith.

The <u>Sally</u> bound on a voyage to Madeira and thence to Havannah or some other port in the West Indies, was taken by a French frigate and the pursuer was kept by the French, in accordance with an arrangement made by the two captains as "ransomer and hostage to the enemy ... for security for £700" which was to be given the French captain for ransom of the ship and cargo. At Port Louise this frigate proving unfit for further service House was put on another French ship en route for France. While lying in a creek off New York harbor, he swam to an English ship lying nearby. After other adventures he arrived in Leith. He brought action for £50 wages and expenses and for £300 as a solatium for "his terrible confinement and other hardships".

AC7/51   **November 15, 1765**

John Ross, merchant in London, and James McGibbon, brewer in Portsburgh, Edinburgh, his trustees, v. William Dunbar of Machriemore in Antigua for £915 11 shillings 6 pence sterling, with interest, on a bill of exchange given for that amount.

AC7/51   **June 3, 1766**

Thomas Dunmore and Company, merchants in Glasgow, v. John Greenlees and Thomas Hardy, merchants in Norfolk, Virginia, under the firm of Greenlees and Hardy, for £527 2 shillings 8 pence for goods received.

AC7/51   **December 9, 1766**

David and Alexander Campbell, merchants in Glasgow, for themselves and the other creditors of Archibald Dunlop, late merchant in Glasgow, now in Virginia, v. Archibald Dunlop for money owing on goods received.

AC7/52   **February 10, 1767**

James Hutton, merchant in Leith, a partner and manager of the Leith Ropery Company, v. Messrs Forest and Blair, merchants in Edinburgh, and Roger Ballingall, shipmaster in Leith, for ropes and sails for a new ship to be built for their use in America.

AC7/52   **July 3, 1767**

Thomas Crawford, merchant in London, presently in Edinburgh, and his trustee John Neall, a merchant in Edinburgh, v. David Freebairn, merchant in Kingston, Jamaica, and William Noble, shipmaster in Port Glasgow, for goods furnished to be sent to Jamaica.

AC7/52   **August 14, 1767**

William Murray, merchant in Edinburgh, v. Donald Edie, shipmaster, and David Loch, merchant in Leith, for money received from Robert Boyd, a merchant in Charleston, for goods shipped to there on the <u>Helen of Leith</u>.

AC7/53   **August 1, 1769**

James Hutton, merchant in Leith, accountant and manager and partner of the Leith Ropery Company, v. Alexander Cunningham and Cornelius Elliot, clerks to the Signet, James Montgomery, His Majesty's Advocate, Andrew Ronaldson of Blairhall, and William Bell, merchant in Leith, for a balance due on ropes and sails purchased for the use of the <u>Edinburgh</u>, which was shipwrecked on a voyage to Jamaica, but insured to her full value. The defendants are the nearest of kin to the deceased Michael Ancrum, merchant in Edinburgh. He and John McLean, deceased, merchant in Kingston, Jamaica, owned the Edinburgh.

AC7/53   April 11, August 18, 1769

Thomas Carnegy, brewer in the Canongate, Edinburgh, v. Archibald McLarty, shipmaster in Greenock. John Welsh, a merchant in Jamaica, had a son by a Janet Chapman; both she and the child lived at the home of the pursuer while Welsh remitted money for their maintainance. Welsh eventually send for Chapman to come to Jamaica as his housekeeper and sent money for this purpose via McLarty of the Britannia.

AC7/53   December 29, 1769

Alexander Kennedy, merchant in Ayr, v. David Hunter, late merchant in Ayr afterwards in Virginia, for goods sold to Mr Hunter and taken by him to Virginia to dispose of. Hunter did this but made no return of his sales to the pursuer.

AC7/53   January 16, 1770

John Kennedy, master and part-owner of the brigantine Carolina and William McCree, merchant in Glasgow, his attorney, v. James Tulloch McFie, mate, John Duncan,

George Scuton, William Potts, Soloman Strong, John Linquist, and Hugh Affan, all late sailors on the <u>Carolina</u>.

The said ship went on a voyage from Liverpool to the coast of Guinea and then to Maryland. There a cargo of tobacco was loaded, the above crew engaged to replace others who had died. On the way back to Liverpool the ship was wrecked and the cargo, except two hogsheads, was too damaged to sell. No freight was earned and consequently no wages were due to the sailors". In Liverpool the crew had Kennedy arrested and he was imprisoned for eight days.

AC7/54   **July 26, 1771**

Messrs Bogle, Sommerville, and Company, merchants in Glasgow, v. James Coulter, Thomas Scott, and John Shortridge, merchants in Glasgow, and Messrs Clay and Midgely, merchants in Liverpool, for cost, freight, etc. on 100 barrels of flour shipped on the <u>Northumberland,</u> Captain Sarrate, by the pursuer's factor Gavin Laurie in Virginia. On arrival in Liverpool, that port being closed in 1769 against the importation of flour, it was put on board another ship and sent to Dublin, which was done without the consent of the owner.

AC7/55   **March 4, 1774**

John Alston, merchant in Glasgow, v. James Hepburn and Joseph Montford, merchants in Cape Fear for

payment for goods furnished to Messrs James Hepburn and Company, merchants in North Carolina.

AC9/2969   **May 1774**

James Hogg v. James Inglis. This case involves breach of contract in that James Inglis jr agreed to ship James Hogg of Borland in Caithness, his family of three and six servants, with 204 emigrants, from Thurso on board the Bachelor of Leith, master Alexander Ramage, to Wilmington, North Carolina, in 1773. Hogg's brother had settled in Wilmington many years earlier and had persuaded his brother to follow him. The ship was late in sailing, leaving Thurso on 14 September 1773, and encountered severe storms forcing it back to Stromness in the Orkney Islands. On October she left Stromness to cross the Atlantic but was again driven back by storms, this time to Vaila Sound in the Shetland Islands where the ship lay storm damaged over the winter. On 29 April 1774 the ship left for Leith to be repaired where James Inglis stated that the voyage was at an end and claimed that he was entitled to the fares paid.

Reference to Mrs Alves, Hogg's mother in law, a passenger; twenty three passengers were discharged in Stromness, eight children aged under 8 years died on the ship in Shetland and eighteen full and ten half passengers left the ship in Shetland; James Hogg with his family and some of the emigrants later sailed from Greenock to Virginia .

The following passengers on the <u>Bachelor of Leith</u>, master Alexander Ramage, bound for North Carolina, were discharged: Alexander Mackay in Stromness, and George Nicol and his wife, George Morgan and his wife, Donald Cattenach and his family, John Ross and his family, William Cattenach, Donald Gunn, George McDonald and William McDonald, were all discharged in the Shetland Islands. The following died on the ship: Alexander McKay's child, John McKay's child, Alexander Gunn's child, John Gunn's child, James Gordon's child, George McKay's child, and George Morgan's child.

AC7/55   **June 3, September 13, 1774 & September 22, 1775**

William Allan, sometime carpenter on the <u>Beverley of Glasgow</u>, and several seamen on the said ship, v. John Graham Baillie, John Gray, Peter or Patrick Mitchell, merchants in Glasgow, and James Millar , merchant in Virginia, for wages due on a voyage on the said ship from the Clyde to Virginia and return.

AC9/2779   **September 26, 1774**

Petition by John Laverock, master of the <u>American Planter of Leith</u> on behalf of himself and the crew of the said ship for unpaid wages for a voyage to the Bay of Honduras and back. The then skipper of the ship,

Captain Robert Alexander, hired John Laverock, James Beveridge mate, Alexander McKay second mate, James Balfour carpenter, Matthew Hunter, Hugh Paterson and James Browne all sailors, David Robertson an apprentice and John Tawse a boy, as crew for the voyage. Captain Robert Alexander died at sea on 3 February 1773 and John Laverock took command.
AC7/55   January 20, 1775

John Dick, carpenter in Airth, v. James Addison jnr., merchant in Bo'ness, for wages due on Patrick Cowan's ship the <u>Christian</u> on a voyage from Airth to Virginia in 1772. Addison is the representative of Cowan deceased.

AC7/55   August 4, 1775

John McKinnon, sometime merchant at the Bay of Honduras, now in London, and William McDonald, Writer to the Signet, his attorney, v. Roger Gale, merchant at the Bay of Honduras.

McKinnon and Gale were partners in the business of logwood traders in Honduras. During the term of their co-partnership all business was to be done to their mutual advantage. Gale, however, brought down a ship from New York laden with goods with which he did a considerable trade, and in similar ways disregarded his agreement. A brigantine of Gale's, the <u>Benjamin of Honduras</u>, while lying in Leith harbour, was seized by the pursuer who brings action for his share in the private transactions.

AC9/2903/2   **January 22, 1776**

James Reid v. William Millar in Wilmington, North
Carolina.

AC7/55   **March 12, 1776**

Duncan Thomson, mariner in Greenock, v. Thomas
Ramsay, shipmaster in Greenock, for damages
sustained in being pressed into service on the ship of
war Salisbury by Ramsay, while on a voyage on the
Peggy to Boston.

AC7/55   **April 2, 1776**

James Reid Smith in Port Glasgow v. William Millar,
shipbuilder in Wilmington, North Carolina, for money due
for materials.

AC7/55   **April 16, June 7, 1776**

James Hamilton, late mate, James Crawford, late
carpenter, and James McKinnon, late sailor, all on
board the Rae Galley v. William Morrison, James Taylor
and Company, merchants in Greenock, for wages due
on a voyage from Greenock to Philadelphia then to

Jamaica thereafter to the Bay of Honduras and back to Greenock.

"Receipt by John Foulis for long boat dated Savannah, Georgia, 4 June 1774"

"Greenock 10 August 1775. We the undersubscribers do hereby certify that we know it to be the custom and practice of ships destined from the Bay of Honduras to call at Cork for orders and their putting in to Cork is never considered as any deviation from the voyage, signed John Buchanan, George Buchanan jnr., and Stephen Rowan."

AC7/55   June 7, 1776

Hugh Ross jnr., silversmith in Tain, v. David Ross, town clerk of Tain, and Charles Ross, late merchant in Tain, now residing at Smithfield, Virginia, for money due.

AC7/55   November 1, 1776

Matthew Squire, commander of <u>HMS Otter</u>, James Wardrop on board the schooner <u>Betsy</u>, a prize, his agent and trustee, with concourse of Mr John Munro, procurator fiscal of the court, v. Thomas Newman, late master of the <u>Betsy</u>, schooner, and all others having interest in it, asking the <u>Betsy</u> to be adjudged his lawful prize and property. The <u>Betsy</u> was bound from Ipswich in Massachusetts Bay for some southern colony when it was captured within the Capes of Virginia.

"These may certify whom it may concern that Thomas
Newman, master of the schooner <u>Betsy</u> burden 50 tons
hath here taken on board said vessel one hogshead of
rum and also two hundred pounds of cash in Continental
bills bound for some of the Southern Colonies for the
purpose of purchasing grain and hath given bond to land
his cargo in some one of the United Colonies, the ports
of Boston and Nantucket excepted, and further the said
Newman is recommended to the good people of the said
colonies by the Committee of this town as a hearty
friend to his country and it is earnestly desired that he
may be assisted in purchasing a cargo as soon as may
be. (signed) David Noyes per order of the Committee of
Correspondence of Ipswih Province of Massachusetts
Bay. Ipswich January 8th, 1776."

The capture was made in accordance with the Act of
Parliament forbidding trade with the revolting colonies.

AC7/56   **July 18, 1777**

James Reid, smith in Port Glasgow, v. William Miller,
shipbuilder in Wilmington, North Carolina, regarding an
unpaid account of £26.8 shillings 8 pence sterling.

AC7/56   **June 6, June 20, July 18, August 22, 1777**

Messrs Hamilton, Wallace, and Company, merchants in
Greenock, v. William Millar, shipbuilder in Wilmington,

North Carolina, for money due for materials purchased, one fourth share in the brigantine <u>Hunter</u>, etc.

AC7/56   **August 1, 1777**

John Fraser, shipbuilder in Newton on Ayr, John Smith, shipmaster there, and James Montgomery, tacksman of the Newton Coal Company, v. Robert Ferguson of Castlehill and David Cochran, now a merchant in Virginia.

The defender failed to fulfill the conditions of the charter party entered into with the pursuer, owners of the brigantine <u>Friendship of Ayr</u> by which they were to take a cargo of coal on the said ship to Virginia and return with a cargo of tobacco or other suitable commodities, paying the pursuer an agreed freight charge. Action is brought for payments due.

AC9/2864   **1777**

Petition by John Glassford, James Gordon, Walter Monteath, merchants in Glasgow, attorneys for John Chinnery, Captain of <u>HMS Daphne</u> and other officers and crew of the said ship, with concourse of John Monro, advocate and procurator fiscal of the High Court of the Admiraly.

The brigantine <u>Elizabeth of Philadelphia</u>, master Thomas Crawford, sailed from Philadelphia with a cargo of tobacco and flour, bound for France in 1776. The ship was captured 20 leagues off Cape Henlopen at the mouth of the Delaware by the <u>Daphne</u> taken to New York and later to the Clyde. Reference to Joseph Steers aged 33, quartermaster, and John Dykes, sailing master, of the <u>Daphne</u>. The manifest of the <u>Elizabeth</u> had been signed by George Bryon prior to sailing. From New York the <u>Elizabeth</u> was under John Dunnet, aged 36, a skipper from Port Glasgow, and Henry Whyte, mate, who sailed the vessel to the Clyde. The <u>Elizabeth of Philadelphia</u> and her cargo were condemned as a prize on 21 November 1777.

AC8/2005/1   1777
AC8/2016/1

An account of the sale of goods at Charleston, South Carolina, by John McKenna and Walter Scott in 1753.

AC9/1591/19   1777

An inventory of the cargo aboard the <u>Elizabeth and Peggy of Leith</u> on a voyage to Carolina in 1753.

AC9/1591/7   1777

Financial records of the <u>Elizabeth and Peggy of Leith</u>, Captain Walter Scott, which sailed from Leith to Charleston, South Carolina, in 1757. Among those on board were Robert Bailey a merchant in Edinburgh,

John McKenna a merchant in Edinburgh who acted as supercargo, and Alexander McDougall an auditor's clerk from the Exchequer in Edinburgh, plus unnamed indentured servants.

AC7/56   **June 30. 1778**

John Elston, writer in Edinburgh, v. John Armstrong, sometime writer in Edinburgh now in Jamaica, Alexander Drysdale, Mrs Isabel Douglas, James Hamilton, Alexander Allan, Henry Arnot, Thomas Brown, Captain David Wood, James Gilkie, Andrew Marshall, James Hay, David Johnston, John Trotter jnr., and Lieutenant Robert Douglas, for money owing.

AC7/58   **April 24, 1778**

John Gilchrist, carpenter, sometime on board the Benjamin of the Bay of Honduras, owned by Roger Gale, a merchant there, and Samuel Watson, one of the procurators of the court, his trustee, v. Roger Gale of the Bay of Honduras for wages due.

AC7/58   **June 19, September 25, 1778**

John Munro, advocate, procurator of the court, v. William Sextroh, late master of the Minerva of Charleston, South Carolina, and his mate.

The ship was captured under the law forbidding trade with the rebellious colonies. It was a trading vessel from Charleston, South Carolina, bound for Gothenborg, Sweden.

Captain George Innes of the <u>Sally of Greenock</u>, on a voyage out to New York "after a very obstinate engagement for the space of three glasses" was taken on April 11 by the <u>Wexford</u>, an American privateer, belonging to Newbury, New England, commander John Fletcher. Some time later the <u>Wexford</u>, Captain Innes being on board the said privateer spoke to the ship <u>Minerva of Charleston</u>, master William Sextroh, bound to Gothenborg, laden with tobacco, rice, indigo, and logwood. Captain Sextroh having complained to the commander of the privateer of the want of men to navigate the <u>Minerva</u>, Captain Fletcher allowed Captain Innes, four of his men and a boy to go on board the <u>Minerva</u> to assist in its navigation. On May 7 Captain Innes, his people, and some of the <u>Minerva</u> crew who joined him, took the command from Captain Sextroh and brought her, with the rest of the crew, fifteen hands and one lady passenger into Greenock, arriving there on May 13.

Admitted as evidence are the invoice of goods, certificate of ownership of the <u>Minerva</u>, and a letter from David Bordeaux of Charleston, whose tobacco was a part of the cargo, to John Vandervolt of Gothenborg, April 4, 1778, in which he states that "such has been the scarcity of dry goods in these United States and particularly in this that they will now bring from ten to fifteen hundred on the European cost. The African

Trade which is at present prohibited, will be in a little time, as soon as the prohibition is taken off, become a branch of commerce of great importance, and as I understand you are considerably connected in that branch of business, I shall take upon me to give you the earliest intelligence after the prohibition ceases".

AC7/56   **June 26, July 10, 1778**

Sommerville, Gordon, and Company, merchants in Glasgow, v. William and Matthew Lewis, planters in Jamaica, for payment on a note, which had been protested, given by the defenders to Captain James Wallace and endorsed by him to the pursuers.

AC7/56   **September 11, 1778**

David Gibb, sometime sailor on board the Jenny, and Thomas Reid, tailor in Bo'ness, his attorney, v. Peter Lawson, merchant in Bo'ness, for wages due on a voyage taken from Cork to the West Indies. Lawson had agreed to insure the partner's wages on this voyage. The Jenny was wrecked on this voyage.

AC7/56   **October 30, 1778**

William Cunningham, merchant in Glasgow, owner of the Prince of Wales and James McLean, commander, with concourse of John Munro, advocate, procurator fiscal of the court, v. Jonathan Clark, commander of the sloop **Eclipse of Baltimore**. While cruising in the Bay of Biscay, the **Prince of Wales** came up with and captured the **Eclipse**, then on her way from Maryland to Bordeaux with a cargo of tobacco.

AC7/57   **April 27, June 11, July 2 1779**

A petition in the name of Alexander Ogilvy, merchant in Leith, part owner of the **John of Leith**, that it may be returned to him.

The **John** was built in New England for some Greenock merchants in 1774 and was for a time used as a transport in government service. About the end of March 1778 it was fitted with a letter of marque, and sailed for New York, but was captured on the way and taken into a New England port. A ship called the **Monmouth** which sailed from Casco Bay, New England, in the past winter bound for France was seized by some of the crew and brought into Glasgow. This ship, they believe, is the **John of Leith**, for which proof will be submitted.

The **Monmouth**, Master William Farris, sailed from Casco Bay, Massachusetts, in January 1779 bound for Nantz, France, during the voyage the mate Allan McKinlay with some of the crew seized the vessel and headed for Scotland, landing at Lochindale, Islay. On 14 March 1779 the ship was brought from there to Glasgow arriving there two days later.

Reference to John Cheever, aged 20, unmarried, late sailor on the <u>Monmouth</u> now in Port Glasgow. Allan McKinlay, aged 26, unmarried, late mate on the <u>Monmouth</u>. George Ross, aged 20, a seaman on the <u>Monmouth</u> formerly on the man o'war <u>Somerset</u>, Captain Orry, which had been driven ashore on Cape Cod where he and the rest of the crew were taken as prisoners to Boston. There he was engaged as a seaman on the <u>Monmouth</u> with the aim of regaining his liberty. All the crew except Joseph Cordes the supercargo, John Sheever, and the cook took part in the mutiny. Alexander Calder, aged 21, unmarried, late seaman on <u>HMS Somerset</u> last of the American ship <u>Monmouth</u>. Alexander Allan, aged 25, unmarried, late seaman on <u>HMS Somerset</u>. Robert Back, aged 42, married, late seaman on <u>HMS Somerset</u> last on the American ship the <u>Monmouth</u>. Allan McKay formerly mate of the <u>Caledonia</u>, owned by Ramsay Howat and Company, which was captured by an American privateer and taken to Newbury where he enrolled on the <u>Monmouth</u>.

AC7/57   **August 27, 1779**

Robert Stewart, commander and part owner of the <u>Tynecastle</u> with concourse of John Munro, advocate, procurator fiscal of the court, v. John Viccary, commander of the sloop <u>Charlotte of Philadelphia</u>. The <u>Tynecastle</u> fitted out with a letter of marque, sailed from the Clyde on 1 July 1779 on a cruise overtook and on 27 July 1779 captured the <u>Charlotte</u> bound for Cadiz loaded with ten hogsheads of tobacco and some staves and took her to Greenock. Pursuer asks that it be adjudged a lawful prize and his property.

Reference to Dougal McLellan, aged 36, First Lieutenant of the Tynecastle, and to Alexander Taylor, aged 20, unmarried, clerk on the said ship.

AC7/57   **September 10, 1779**

A petition of William Morrison and Company, merchants in Greenock, owners of the brig Hero, letter of marque, for proofs of her capturing etc., determining salvage due to them.

The Hero, master James Morris, retook the Elephant, which had been in government service at New York and had been captured by the Miflin a Boston privateer, and brought it to the Clyde on 20 June 1779. The Elephant, under an American master ... Smith and thirteen American seamen, had been bound for France with merchandise when taken by the Hero.

Reference to Leonard J. Anson, aged 36, unmarried, James Dewsbie, aged 30, unmarried, both of the Elephant, John Goudie, aged 25, married, second mate of the Hero, William Brown, aged 18, unmarried, from Greenock, seaman on the Hero and on the Elephant.

AC7/58   **October 8, 1779**

Alexander Simpson, a merchant tailor in Edinburgh, v.
Doctor Dennis Dorsey, sometime student of physic in
the University of Edinburgh, now in America, for money
owing.

AC7/57   **January 28, 1780**

Neill Campbell, shipmaster in Port Glasgow, v. Charles
Wightman and Archibald Smith, merchants in Tobago,
for money due on a promissary note. They failed to
fulfill their agreement to deliver to Captain Peter
Campbell of the brig <u>John</u>, produce to the value of £279
8 shillings 11 pence sterling for which their note was
given.

AC7/57   **April 21, 1780**

James Scott of Scalloway, and David Forbes, writer in
Edinburgh, his agent and trustee, v. Lieutenant Charles
Hunter of Burnside, late of the <u>Africa</u>, now of the <u>Jupiter</u>
tender. In a condemnation suit in the High Court of the
Admiralty against Moses Grinnell, master of the <u>Sally
and Becky of Boston</u> the defender was ordered to pay
to the pursuer, as having been first in possession of the
said ship before he was forcibly turned out by the
defender, £200 sterling, which he has so far failed to do.

AC7/58, 59

June 23, November 28, 1780
January 17, February 28, 1783

Robert Lee, merchant in Greenock, as factor for and in name and behalf of the masters, officers and crew of the privateer Endeavour of Glasgow, v. Messrs William Thomson and Whyte.

The Endeavour, under the command of Captain Alexander Taylor, made a prize of La Jeune Agathe bound from St Domingo to France. The defenders, owners of the privateer, have refused to pay the pursuer the amounts due from this capture and awarded by the courts.

AC7/57

August 11, 1780

Captain John Hastie, commander of the privateer Hawke of Greenock, and John Kippen, merchant in Greenock, for himself and other owners of the said privateer, with the concourse of the procurator fiscal, v. Abraham Newell, mate of the American vessel Lively of Massachusetts.

The Lively of Massachusetts, 30 tons, master Ebenezer Stocks, en routs from Newbury, Massachusetts, to Guadaloupe, with a cargo of fish, staves, and shingles, was captured in June by the Hawke of Greenock. Pursuers ask to have it condemned as a prize.

Reference to Michael Dupuy former master of the Lively of Newburyport, a square sterned vessel built in

Massachusetts in 1771, owned by John Coffin Jones of Newburyport and Joseph Lee of Marblehead. Robert McKirdy, aged 23, unmarried, mate of the Hawke. George Grieve, aged 17, late mariner on the Hawke

AC7/57   **September 15, 1780**

Captain John Hastie, commander of the privateer Hawke of Greenock, and John Kippen, merchant in Greenock, for himself and other owners of the Hawke, with concourse of the procurator fiscal, John Munro, v. Samuel Lord, late mate of the brigantine Jolly Tar, (built in Bordeaux 1777) now in Greenock, which the pursuers ask to be condemned as a prize.

The Jolly Tar, a 100 ton brigantine, master William Clark, was captured while en route from Piscataqua, New Hampshire, to St Martin's in the West Indies, and brought to the Clyde. She was owned by Samuel Gardner in Portsmouth, New Hampshire, and laden with 36,000 feet of board, plank, and joists, 10,000 hogshead of staves, and 30,000 shingles. Reference to Nathaniel Barber, Naval Officer at Piscataqua, New Hampshire.

AC7/57   **November 21, 1780**

Robert Dunmore and Company, merchants in Glasgow, v. William Dawes Quarrel, in Hanover, Jamaica, for money owing.

AC7/58   **January 16, 1781**

Francis Russel, late chief mate of the brigantine <u>Chance of Greenock</u>, presently at Ardeer in the parish of Stevenston, Ayrshire, v. William and James Donald, merchants, for themselves and partners under the firm of William and James Donald and Company, and John Campbell and ...... Thomson, merchants and copartners under the firm of Campbell and Thomson, all of Greenock, for the salvage due him for recapturing the <u>Chance</u> from the sloop <u>Providence</u>, a Boston privateer. In August 1777 the <u>Chance,</u> a 200 ton vessel, master John Simpson, with a crew of 8 men and a boy, sailed for a voyage to North America and the West Indies and return, and arrived in Mobile in April 1778.

AC7/58   **January 29, April 10, 1781**

James Gemmell and Company, merchants in Greenock, v. Robert Miller, late master of the <u>Nancy of Leith,</u> for money owing for freight etc., due on a charter party agreement made in St Kitts between John Dean, master of the brigantine <u>Ajax</u> the <u>Nancy</u>'s cargo of sugar, rum, and cotton, and bring it to London. Dean placed Miller

in charge of the <u>Ajax</u> who performed the journey, but did not make the necessary payments to the pursuers who owned the brigantine.

AC7/58   **April 24, 1781**

Messrs Hamilton, McIver and Company, merchants in Greenock, agents for the privateer <u>Tarleton of Greenock</u> and part owners, for themselves and the other owners, and Alexander Taylor, master of the said privateer, with concourse of John Munro, procurator fiscal of the court, v. Captain George Buchanan, commander of the American ship <u>Tom Lee of Baltimore</u>, asking that it be adjudged a prize. The <u>Tom Lee</u>, which had been built in Bear Creek, Baltimore County, Maryland, during 1780, was laden with 140 hogsheads of tobacco, when captured en route to Nantes, France. The <u>Tom Lee</u> was owned by Archibald Buchanan, the master was John Buchanan aged 37, the First Lieutenant was William Coward aged 25, and the sailing master was William Smith aged 22. It had a passenger on board, a John Lewis aged 22, when it was captured on 23 March 1781.

AC7/58   **September 21,1781**

John Margetson, merchant in London, Messrs Ramsay, Williamson and Company, merchants in Leith, his attornies, with concourse of John Munro, advocate, procurator fiscal of the High Court of the Admiralty, v.

Thomas Skinner, late chief mate on board the brigantine <u>Gustavus of Philadelphia</u>, asking that the <u>Gustavus</u> may be adjudged a prize.

The <u>Gustavus</u>, laden with tobacco, beef, and pork and bread for sea stores while en route from Philadelphia to Marstrand in Sweden and return, was captured on its return voyage by the brig <u>Lively</u>, fitted as a privateer, Willis Marshall, commander, and owned by the pursuers.

Merchandise sent by Henry Greig in Gothenborg and by Charles Soderstrom to Samuel Inglis and Company, John Strummely, John Leary and Company, Robert Morrison and William Bingham, all in Philadelphia.

AC9/2975   1781

James Margetson, merchant in London, and other owners of the privateer <u>Lively of London,</u> Ramsay, Williamson and Company, merchants in Leith, their attorneys, with concourse of John Monro, procurator fiscal of the Court v. Thomas Skinner, First Mate of the American brigantine <u>Gustavus</u>.

The <u>Gustavus of Philadelphia</u>, Captain George Fleming, had sailed from Philadelphia with a cargo of tobacco bound for Marstrand in Sweden in November 1780, on her return voyage, laden with tea and dry goods, she was taken north of the Shetland Islands by the <u>Lively</u>, Captain Willis Machell, and taken to Leith. Reference to Samuel Inglis, George Ord, Robert Morris, Thomas Willing and William Dingham, all merchants in

Philadelphia; Lieutenant Jonathan Dixon, James Boyd, aged 20, master's mate, of the <u>Lively</u>; Nathan Church, second mate, and Herman Jacobsen, bosun of the <u>Gustavus</u>.

| AC9/2978 | September 1781 |
| AC7/58 | October 19, 1781 |

John Margetson, merchant in London, Ramsay, Williamson and Company, merchants in Leith, his attorneys, with concourse of John Monro, advocate, procurator fiscal of the Court. Margetson, and other owners of the brig <u>Lively of London</u>, a privateer, master Willis Machell, captured the brigantine <u>Beckey and Harriat of Boston</u>, a 80 ton square sterned vessel, built in Newbury, Massachusetts, in 1776, commander Moses Grinnell, north of the Shetland Islands bound from Amsterdam to Boston, Massachusetts, with goods shipped by John De Newfville for Isaac Sears and other Boston merchants, and was subsequently taken to the port of Fraserburgh. The <u>Beckey and Harriat</u> with an eight man crew, had cleared Boston on 31 January 1781, and set sail from there on 15 February 1781. Reference to William Harrison, aged 32, First Lieutenant of the <u>Lively</u>, and William Dickson, aged 20, captain's servant.

AC7/58   January 16, 1781

Francis Russell, late chief mate of the brigantine <u>Chance of Greenock</u>, v. William and James Donald, merchants in Greenock, and Campbell and Thomson, merchants in Greenock.

A case concerning salvage due for the re-capture of the above brigantine **Chance** from the sloop **Providence** a Boston privateer

AC7/58   **June 15, 1781**

John Ross, late merchant at Loch Broom, now in Nova Scotia, presently residing in Edinburgh, v. Mr Joseph Munro, minister of the Gospel at Edderton, for money owing on rum purchased from the pursuer.

John Ross had a cargo of rum on board the **Peggy,** master William Mitchell, bound from St Croix in the West Indies to North Faro. The **Peggy,** however, was wrecked at Torrisdale, Sutherland, where Mr Munro intromitted with and purchased some of the rum.

AC7/58   **June 21, 1781**

Andrew Thomson, a merchant in Glasgow, v. William Snodgrass, sometime merchant in Glasgow now in North America, concerning a contract of co-partnery dated 23 October 1776 between Andrew Thomson and William Snodgrass, merchants in Glasgow now in North America, and by George McCaull a merchant in Glasgow, James Crawford and Samuel Crawford merchants in Greenock, and Archibald Bryde plus John Snodgrass, merchants in Virginia. Under the contract

Archibald Bryce was to manage the business in Richmond, Virginia, and John Snodgrass, was to manage to business in Goochland, Virginia.

AC7/58 **October 5, 1781**

James Margetson, merchant in London, and Messrs Ramsay, Williamson and Company, merchants in Leith, with concourse of John Monro, advocate, procurator fiscal of the court, v. William Gibbons, master, and Thomas Cleghorn, mate of the snow Four Friends of Boston, asking that she be adjudged a prize.

The brig Lively of London, fitted as a privateer, Willis Marshall, commander, off Shetland, captured the Four Friends, on 6 September 1781, laden with dry goods en routs from Amsterdam to Boston. The snow Sara and Rebecca, now called the Four Friends, was bought by William Gibson in Amsterdam for James Bowdoin jnr., Benjamin Clark, Jonathan Mason, and Herman and Andrew Brimmer, merchants in Boston. Reference to John Tufts a passenger on the Four Friends from Amsterdam bound for Boston, and to Christopher Smollett, bosun.

AC7/58 **October 19, 1781**

James Margetson, merchant in London, and Messrs Ramsay, Williamson and Company, merchants in Leith, his attorneys, with concourse of John Monro, advocate, procurator fiscal of the court, v. Moses Grinnell, late commander of the brigantine **Becky and Harriot of Boston,** asking that she may be adjudged a prize.

The **Becky and Harriot** carried to Amsterdam a cargo of flax seed, pot and pearl ashes, elephants' teeth, and sassafras. On her return journey, laden with dry goods she was captured by the **Lively,** owned by the pursuers.

AC9/3032   1781

Francis Russell, late mate of the brigantine **Chance**, v. William and James Donald, merchants in Greenock, & Campbell and Thomson, merchants in Greenock.

The ship **Chance,** master John Simpson, was when on her outward voyage captured at Mobile Point during May 1778 by the Americans who had come down the Mississippi in canoes, however a number of gentlemen and seamen from Mobile in the **John Weter**, Captain Roberts retook her and brought her back to Mobile Bay in company with the sloop of war **Hound.** The **Chance** then sailed to Jamaica. On 25 November 1778 she joined a convoy which sailed from Port Royal, Jamaica, which included the **Cupid**, the **Greenwich**, and the **Nabob**, bound for the Clyde. On the 14 December 1778 the **Chance** became detached from the convoy in the Gulf of Florida and was taken at 37 degrees north 55 degrees west at three o'clock in the afternoon by the sloop **Providence**, Captain Patrick Rathbon, which was on a cruise from Boston. A prize crew was put aboard which included James Adam, the prizemaster, Daniel

Ritchie, the chief mate, and seven sailors. Among the prize crew was Daniel Turner who Russell had known in New York. On 1 January 1779 Francis Russell, first mate, William Hastie, second mate, John Burton, an 18 year old apprentice, Daniel Turner, Daniel Horn, and an Italian American Codata Dusin retook the ship. Later they were joined by Nicolas Massey, Thomas Farming and the chief mate Daniel Ritchie, and the ship was brought back to Scotland.

AC7/58   **June 21, 1782**

Andrew Thomson, merchant in Glasgow, v. William Snodgrass, sometime merchant in Glasgow now in North America, for money owing as a partner of a business.

Andrew Thomson, William Snodgrass, George McCall, merchant in Glasgow, James and Samuel Crawford, merchants in Greenock, with Archibald Bryce and John Snodgrass, merchants in Virginia, on 25 February 1778 formed a copartnership for carrying on trade in stores in Richmond and in Goochland, Virginia.

AC7/58   **August 9, 1782**

Dennistoun, Brown and Company, merchants in Glasgow, v. James Campbell, a merchant in St George's, Grenada.

AC7/58   **September 4, 1782**

Isobel Syme in Greenock v. Archibald Greig, late
commander of the <u>Ceres</u>, for wages due to and
belongings of her husband, now deceased, on a voyage
from St Kitts to Greenock in 1779/1780.

AC7/58   **December 13, 1782**

Robert Eason, a merchant in Stirling, v. Robert Kerr,
master of the <u>Quebec of Greenock</u> during a voyage to
Grenada in 1780.

AC7/60   **February 1, 1783**

William Lowdon, master of the <u>Mally of Dumfries</u> and
John Sloan, vintner in Kirkcudbright, v. David Blair,
mate, Mathew Johnston bosun, also Robert Drinan,
Alexander Blair, and William Wilson, all sailors on the
<u>Mally</u>, concerning wages due on a voyage to America in
1776. The vessel had been freighted by Kirkpatrick and
Currie, merchants in Dumfries, for a voyage from
Kirkcudbright to Halifax, Nova Scotia, New York, and
then Pictou, Nova Scotia. At Pictou when she was
being loaded with timber for the return voyage the ship
was captured by an American privateer and taken to
Veritbay(?) in November 1776. Later she was rescued
by British forces and sailed to Charlottetown, Prince
Edward Island. On 12 April 1777 she returned to Pictou
and resumed loading timber and left there bound for
Scotland on 7 July 1777.

Robert Easson, merchant in Stirling, v. Robert Kerr, master of the <u>Quebec of Greenock</u> for wages due for a voyage to Quebec in April 1782.

AC7/59   June 24, 1783

Alexander Ogilvy, merchant in Leith, for himself and other agents of the <u>Sally and Becky of Boston</u>, prize to <u>HMS Africa,</u> v. Lieutenant Charles Hunter, late commander of the <u>Africa</u>, master George Whitehead, Thomas Thomson, pilot, James Hyslop, surgeon, Ralph Cook, master's mate, Anne Wallace, relict of David Kirkcaldy, midshipman, all on board the said <u>Africa</u> tender, concerning the proper distribution and time of payment of the prize money due to the defenders for the capture of the <u>Sally and Becky.</u>

AC7/59   June 27, 1783

Archibald Graham, late carpenter on board the <u>Thomas and Betsey of Leith</u>, v. John Stein, shipmaster in Kincardine, and Janet Stein, relict of Thomas Yelton, shipmaster there, for balance of wages due on a voyage from Leith to Jamaica.

AC7/60   August 12, 1785

John Sheddan and Company, sometime merchants in Virginia now in Glasgow, v. Isobel Campbell in Glasgow, widow of George Logan sometime merchant in Norfolk, Virginia. On 8 August 1775 the pursuer insured the sloop <u>Agatha</u>, master Christopher Wilson, for a voyage from Norfolk to Tobago and return. On the return journey she was captured by an American privateer or man'o'war, Captain Barro, of Hampton, Virginia, and taken to Petersburg, Virginia, where she was condemned as a prize vessel. Robert Gilmour, merchant sometime of Norfolk, Virginia, now in London, and Robert Dunmore, merchant in Glasgow, only surviving partners of Logan, Gilmour and Company, together with Isabel Campbell or Logan in Glasgow, relict of George Logan, merchant in Norfolk, Virginia, deceased, were found to be liable.

AC7/59   **August 27, 1783**

James Clark, shoemaker in Edinburgh, v. James Penman, merchant in St Augustine, East Florida, James Stewart in London, and Donald Dean, a merchant in Inverness, for money owing. Penman's debt is £701 7 shillings for a consignment of shoes received in August 1779 which had been shipped on the <u>Betsey</u>, master James Temple, in March 1779.

AC7/62   **December 5, 1783**

John Ross, merchant at Lochbroom, now in the province of Nova Scotia, presently in Edinburgh, v. Captain Charles Gordon of Shelpick. In late 1774 or early 1775 the pursuer John Ross, was returning from

St Croix in the West Indies on the <u>Peggy</u>, master William Mitchell, with a cargo of rum bound for North Faroe, when the ship was wrecked near Torrisdale on the coast of Sutherland. Ross claimed that Gordon purchased some of the rum, amounting to 21 ankers of double rum, that was saved on 11 January 1775, but had failed to pay. Gordon claimed that the rum was a gift in appreciation of help given after the shipwreck.

AC7/61   February 20, 1784

Andrew Watson, merchant in Greenock, v. John Carmalt, merchant there, concerning insurance on the <u>Mercury</u>, master Hannibal Lush, bound for Tortula in 1782.

AC7/61   March 5, 1784

Gavin Kemp and Company, merchants in Leith, v. William Glen, merchant in Forganhall, Falkirk, David Paterson insurance broker in Edinburgh, William Fettes and George Finlay merchants in Edinburgh, James Clark shoemaker in Edinburgh, and Thomas Johnston saddler in Edinburgh. A case concerning the insurance of goods on the ship <u>Friendship</u> in 1782. On 18 November 1782 the <u>Friendship</u>, master Duncan McRob, sailed from the Clyde bound for Antigua. The ship was severely storm damaged at sea and on 24 January 1783 was captured by the American privateer <u>The Commander</u>. All on board, with the exception of Archibald Campbell part-owner, and George McCulloch a passengers, were transferred to the privateer. On 26 January 1783 <u>HMS Enterprize</u>, Captain William Carnegie, appeared and the privateer released the <u>Friendship</u> and quickly made for Martinique. The <u>Friendship</u> was then taken by the Royal Navy to Island Harbor, Antigua, arriving there on 29 January 1783. Reference to John Hardcastle, notary public in Antigua and Deputy Secretary of the island.

AC7/61   **March 17, 1784**

Robert Bog, merchant in Greenock, v. Gabriel Lang, merchant in Greenock, concerning insurance on a consignment of shoes and other goods on board the brigantine <u>New York</u>, Captain Farley, which was cast away on the coast of America during a voyage from the Clyde to New York in September 1783.

AC16/5/88-473   **May 19, 1784**

John McIver and Archibald McCallum found guilty of fraudulently casting away the <u>Endeavour</u> on her voyage to Halifax and the <u>New York</u> by running her ashore off the coast of America. The <u>Endeavour</u> was taken by an American privateer before she was cast away. They were found guilty as to the <u>Endeavour</u> but acquitted as to the <u>New York</u> and were banished from Scotland for life.

AC16/i4/250-420   **June 11, 1784**

James Herdman, merchant in Greenock, and others,
owners of the <u>Peggy</u> and the <u>New York</u>, were found
guilty of fraudulently sinking the <u>Peggy</u> off the coast of
Ireland and the <u>New York</u> off the coast of America, and
were ordered to be pilloried and then banished from
Scotland for life. William Clark, a merchant in Greenock,
found guilty of recording goods which he had put
aboard the <u>Peggy</u> in the knowledge that she was to be
cast away, was outlawed.

AC7/61   **June 25, 1784**

Hugh Dunlop, merchant in Kilmarnock, Ayrshire, v.
Richard Allan jnr., Andrew Houstoun, and James
McDowall, merchants in Glasgow, concerning insurance
on goods shipped from the Clyde on the <u>Castle Semple</u>,
Captain Alexander McCurly, bound via Cork for St Kitts.
Certain merchandise was destined for Alexander Fairnie
in St Martin's, and had to be delivered to Robert
Crawford, a merchant in St Kitts. During the voyage the
skipper learnt of the capture of St Kitts by the French
and consequently headed for Antigua. However the
merchandise for Fairnie which had been deposited in
John Ross's store in Antigua was accidentally
destroyed.

AC9/3184 1784

Hay Campbell, HM Advocate and John Monro, procurator fiscal of the High Court of the Admiralty, v. James Herdman, merchant in Greenock, Duncan Clark, merchant in Edinburgh, and David Thomson, merchant in Greenock, owner of the <u>Peggy of Greenock</u> charged with wilfully casting the said sloop away, and also the brigantine <u>New York</u>. The <u>Peggy</u> had been on a trading voyage to Guernsey and Antigua in December 1782. Reference to Archibald Whyte, master of the <u>Peggy</u> and to William Folley, master of the <u>New York.</u>

AC9/3182 1784

Cunningham, Dougal and Company, merchants in Glasgow, v. John Wardrop, distiller in Dunipace.

John Wardrop took action on behalf of his son Ralph Wardrop, and other members of the crew of the <u>Hannah</u> for wages due. The <u>Hannah</u>, a brigantine, master Thomas Wilkie, sailed in 1779 from Port Glasgow bound for Cork, New York, Jamaica, and return. En route it was captured by an American privateer. The crew included Raph Wardrop, Alexander Fairie, William Mitchell, Robert Drummond, William Weir, James Wilkie, James Ryburn, John Fleming, Archibald Buchan, John Christie, Duncan Johnston, Daniel Cameron, and John Smith.

AC9/184   **1784**

Hay Campbell, HM Advocate, and John Monro,
procurator fiscal of the High Court of the Admiralty, v.
James Herdman, merchant in Greenock, and Duncan
Clark, merchant in Edinburgh, and David Thomson,
merchant in Greenock, owner of the <u>Peggy of Greenock</u>
charged with wilfully casting away the said sloop and
also the brigantine <u>New York</u>. Reference to Archibald
White, master of the <u>Peggy</u> and William Farley, master
of the <u>New York.</u>

The <u>Peggy</u> had been on a trading voyage to Guernsey
and Antigua in December 1782.

AC7/60   **March 11, 1785**

Adam Dawson, distiller and farmer in Barrington, v.
William Anderson, Patrick Robb, and William Morrison,
all in Greenock, concerning an agreement to transport
emigrants from Greenock on the <u>Liberty</u>, master
William Walker, to New York, dated 29 May 1784. The
emigrants listed were – William Anderson, Patrick Robb,
William Morrison, Alexander Caddel, James Maxwell,
Colin Maxwell, Peter Doig, Robert Ferguson, John
Paterson, Margaret Kerr spouse of said Patrick Robb,
Elizabeth Robb, Margaret Robb, Janet Robb, Isobel
Robb, James Robb, William Robb, Ann Robb, Patrick
Robb jnr., Peter Stewart, William Robertson, John Lyon,
Walter Fisher, his spouse and five others.

AC7/60   July 8, 1785

Gavin Alston and Company, merchants in Greenock, v. James and Patrick Hunter and Company, merchants in Port Glasgow, James and Robert Donald, Simon Fraser, John Murchy and David Pagan, merchants in Virginia, joint partners.

AC9/3253   July 9, 1785

George McCall, insurance broker in Glasgow, v. John Longmuir, merchants in Glasgow, and Robert Peacock, merchant in Port Glasgow, re insurance of £503 sterling on goods shipped on the <u>Terry</u>, master Thomas Dolson, from Port Glasgow to Hampton Roads, in America, from there transported in small boats to Oxford, in 1784.

AC9/3244   1785

John Gilchrist, a carpenter journeyman in Dysart, Fife, sometime aboard the <u>Benjamin of the Bay of Honduras</u>, owned by Roger Gale merchant at the Bay of Honduras, and his trustee Samuel Watson, v. said Roger Gale.

Claim for unpaid wages of £18 - 4 shillings due from 1 January 1773 to 9 August 1773, on voyage under Captain John Laverock and subsequently Captain Christopher Gale.

AC7/62   **October 4, 1786**

Dougal Ritchie and Company, merchants in Greenock, v. Andrew McKenzie, late merchant in Greenock now in Dominica. Case concerning insurance on the sloop Hanna from Tilling Bay to the Clyde.

AC7/62   **May 30, 1787**

William Fleming, merchant in Cumnock, Ayrshire, v. James Woods, merchant from America now in Ayr, concerning a consignment of 156 pairs of shoes and other goods sent to Virginia in 1774 to be sold by Woods.

AC7/62   **July 20, 1787**

Steele, Jamieson, Lyon and Company, merchants in Port Glasgow, v. David Elliot, merchant in Greenock. Case concerning insurance on commodities aboard the Jessie, master Neil Campbell, from Glasgow via Cork to Jamaica, which was captured by a privateer.

AC7/63   **December 7, 1787**

Alexander Houstoun and Company, merchants in Glasgow, v. William Calhoun of Kenmure and other merchants in Glasgow. The case concerned the Anne,

master John McNeil, which sailed from Jamaica with a cargo of 12 hogsheads of sugar , in convoy bound for Glasgow, escored by <u>HMS Ramillies</u> on 4 July 1782. The <u>Anne</u> was damaged in a collision at sea but was repaired, however she fell behind and on 5 September 1782 was captured by the brigantine <u>Marshal of New London, Connecticut</u>, an American privateer, master Charles Bulkeley and taken to New London, where the captain and crew were imprisoned.

AC7/62   **April 9, 1788**

Robert Scott, merchant in Glasgow, v. Donald Morrison, gabartman in Greenock. On 15 January 1788 the pursuer sent 12 bales of Osnaburgs to the Broomielaw, Glasgow, to be put on a gabart and transported to Greenock, from there to Liverpool and thence to America. The goods were damaged in transit when in the hands of Morrison and requires to be recompensed.

AC7/62   **June 20, 1788**

James Ritchie and Company, merchants in Glasgow, v. Andrew Jack, George Bogle, Robert Dunlop, and John Gordon, all merchants in Glasgow, concerning insurance paid on the brig <u>Industry</u> bound from Virginia to Havre de Grace in France in September 1786.

AC7/62   **November 25, 1788**

John Inglis, merchant in Glasgow, v. James Lyon and Company, merchants in Kingston, Jamaica, and William Gibson.

AC7/63   **December 19, 1788**

John Alston jnr., merchant in Glasgow, v. Duncan Smith, ship carpenter in Greenock, owner of the brigantine Elizabeth and Thomas. The case concerned money given on 5 November 1787 by Robert Liddell of Baltimore, Maryland, to Thomas Adair, master of the Elizabeth and Thomas, to be delivered on arrival in Glasgow to Walter Ewing, merchant there. The money included 220 new dollars, 138 old dollars, 97 French half crowns, 150 English shillings, 27.5 Johannes, 72 English guineas, 17 English half-guineas.

AC7/63   **November 13, 1789**

Archibald and James Robertson and Company, merchants in Greenock, v. John Land, merchant in Greenock. The case pertained to James Gammel, a merchant in Glasgow, who instructed his correspondents in Virginia to ship tobacco in 1788 on the Fanny of Greenock, master George Henderson, via England to Rotterdam in Holland. The tobacco was duly sent from the Rappahannock River to York River where it was loaded in the <u>Fanny</u> for shipment via Hull, England, to the Netherlands, however the ship was lost at sea.

AC7/64   **1790**

Thomas Boyd, cooper in Ayr, owner of the sloop <u>Peggy of Ayr</u>, v. Andrew Hamilton, merchant in Glasgow, and James Findlay, formerly a merchant in Glasgow now in Jamaica, regarding a policy of insurance on the above ship.

AC7/64   **1790**

James Gammel, merchant in Greenock, v. Michael Wallace, merchant in Halifax, Nova Scotia, concerning money due for goods supplied during the 1780s. Some of them had been distributed in Newfoundland, New York, St Eustatia, Antigua and St Kitts, via Liverpool, Nova Scotia. Reference to the brigantine <u>Dublin</u>, the <u>Lucretia,</u> the brigantine <u>Lucretia</u> and the <u>Glencairn.</u>

AC7/64   **June 18, 1790**

James Paterson and Company, merchants in Greenock, v. John Duguid, a merchant in Glasgow, concerning a trading voyage of the <u>Friendship</u>, master Adam Corsan, from Greenock to Charleston, South Carolina, and return in May 1787.

AC7/64   **November 26, 1790**

John Fullarton, late master of the brigantine <u>Betty of Port Glasgow</u>, resident in Crawforddykes v. Ramsay & Stewart, merchants in Port Glasgow, owners of the vessel. Case concerned with unpaid expenses concerned in the voyage of the <u>Betty</u>, Captain Fullarton, during a voyage from Port Glasgow via Waterford to St Lucia and St Thomas in the West Indies in 1782.

AC7/68   **January 20, 1792**

George Robertson, merchant in Greenock, v. John Campbell, late of Dominica, now in Glasgow, regarding a bill of exchange.

AC7/68   **January 20, 1792**

Stott and Davidson in Petersburg, Virginia, and their attornies Alexander McCaul and John Riddell, merchants in Glasgow, v. Robert Gilmour, merchant in Norfolk, Virginia, presently forth of Scotland, Robert Dunmore and Andrew Blackburn, merchants in Glasgow, and Isabella Campbell in Glasgow, relict of the deceased George Logan, sometime in Norfolk, Virginia.

Case concerned the brigantine <u>John</u>, master John Duncan, which was insured on 3 August 1775 by

Alexander Love in Norfolk, Virginia, for a voyage from there to Hispaniola and then return to North Carolina.

On 1 December 1775 the vessel left Cape Nicola Mole on the return voyage bound for Occacock, North Carolina, and on 18 December was anchored off Cape Hatteras. John Baine, the pilot for Hatteras, came on board on 24 December and took charge of the ship but the ship ran aground. John Duncan and the whole of the crew had to abandon ship. Later on January 14, 1776 John Duncan appeared before Thomas Jones, Notary Public in Edenton, North Carolina, stating that Logan, Gilmour and Company were liable to Alexander Love for £400 Virginia currency.

AC7/68   June 1, 1792

Stott and Donaldson in Petersburg, Virginia, and their attornies Alexander McCaul and John Riddell, merchants in Glasgow, v. Robert Gilmour, merchant in Norfolk, Virginia, presently forth of Scotland, Robert Dunmore and Andrew Blackburn, merchants in Glasgow, Isabella Campbell, relict of George Logan, sometime in Norfolk, Virginia.

The case evolved around an insurance policy subscribed to in Norfolk on 3 August 1775 on the brigantine John, master John Duncan, by Alexander Love in Norfolk, Virginia, for a voyage from there to Hispaniola and back to North Carolina. On December 1, 1775 the ship sailed from Cape Nicola Mole on the return voyage bound for Occacock, North Carolina, and

on 18 December it lay at anchor off Hatteras. John
Baine, the pilot for Hatteras, came on board on 24
December and took charge of the vessel. However the
ship ran aground and the captain and crew had to
abandon ship. Later, on 14 January 1776, John Duncan
made a statement to Thomas Jones, notary public in
Edenton, North Carolina, indicating that Logan, Gilmour
and Company were liable to pay Alexander Love the
sum of £400 Virginia currency.

AC7/67   **May 15, 1794**

John Shiells, surgeon in Edinburgh, v. Alexander Kerr,
late millwright in Edinburgh, now in Jamaica.

AC7/66   **May 30, 1794**

John Biggan and James Tait, v. Hugh Brown, master
and part owner of the brigantine Recovery of Belfast .
In September 1793 a group of prospective emigrants in
Ireland contracted with Hugh Brown to be transported
from Belfast to Charleston, South Carolina. The ship
duly sailed with the passengers on board but almost
immediately it was obvious that the ship was not only
unseaworthy but there was insufficient food for the
voyage and that the crew was under-strength. The
vessel sailed to Loch Ryan in Scotland where the crew
deserted and the captain was unable to recruit a new
crew, thus the voyage was abandoned. The passengers

sued for recompense. The emigrants listed were John Biggan, John Herron, James McSpedden, Martha Cockburn, all from County Down, Alexander Newall and David Strain from County Monaghan, James Tait, David Clyde, Samuel Armstrong, Robert Calbart, Mary Pillan, Agnes Black, Samuel Skene, and William Stewart, all from County Antrim. Reference also to Mary Polling in South Carolina.

AC7/64   **October 24, 1794**

John Stewart, merchant in Port Glasgow, v. Alexander Ritchie, sometime shipmaster in Greenock now in Philadelphia, re unpaid debts dating from 1787.

AC7/66   **October 24, 1794**
AC7/67   **December 5, 1794**

John Stewart, a merchant in Greenock, v. Alexander Ritchie, sometime shipmaster in Greenock now resident in Philadelphia, re an unpaid account.

AC7/67   **May 27, 1795**

John Montgomery, a merchant in Port Glasgow, late in Tortula. Montgomery purchased a captured French brigantine La Fleur in Guadaloupe but before it could be condemned as a prize by Archibald Glaister, Judge of the Vice Admiralty Court of Tortula, the French attacked the town of Grande Terre and stopped the court proceedings. The petitioner left the island on the said vessel and headed for Antigua where it was loaded with sugar bound for Port Glasgow in September. Montgomery wanted the ship officially condemned and presented tow certificates to the court. One of them was a receipt issued by John W. Porter establishing that John Montgomery, a merchant in Tortula, had bought a prize ship the 200 ton brigantine La Fleur, and the other had been subscribed to in Basseterre, Guadaloupe, by Lieutenant Colonel Blundell the Commanding Officer and Governor stating that the ship was legally entitled to be registered at any port in His Majesty's dominions, dated 18 June 1794 and a permit issued to Hugh Paterson master of the brigantine La Fleur to leave Guadaloupe and sail to Antigua, dated 19 June 1794.

AC7/67   **July 17, 1795**

David Paterson, an insurance broker in Edinburgh, v. William Grinlay, a broker in Leith, and James Campbell, a flaxdresser in Edinburgh, regarding insurance on merchandise on the Hopewell Captain Ross, from Honduras to Leith.

AC7/69   **November 13, 1795**

Captain Archibald McNeill, shipmaster in Greenock, v. Roger Stewart, merchant, and Robert Stewart, shipmaster, both in Greenock, concerning voyages of the **Elizabeth of Greenock** from Greenock to Virginia and back.

AC7/67   **November 13, 1795**

Scott and Smith, insurance brokers in Edinburgh, v. Peter Cunningham, goldsmith in Edinburgh, and Muschet Gilchrist, shoemaker in Glasgow, concerning insurance on the **Mary**, Captain Blain, from the Clyde to Jamaica.

AC7/69   **August 5, 1796**

Gavin Young and Company, merchants in London, v. Alexander Campbell, late of Tobago now in Campbelltown, Argyll, regarding a bill of exchange.

AC7/71   **October 6, 1797**

Archibald Crockatt, master of the **Armisted of New York** and Nathan Wilson, writer in Greenock, v. James Gardner, late of New York, now in Glasgow.

AC7/70   **December 12, 1797**

Petition by Jonathan Titcomb, master of the brigantine **Merry of Newburyport** in North America.

In March 1797 the <u>Merry</u> sailing from Hull to
Philadelphia was wrecked on the Sands of Forvie, ten
miles south west of Buchan Ness. The cargo was
unloaded and the ship towed to Aberdeen in May 1797.
Titcomb had advised the owners and had requested
funds to repair the wrecked ship and to resume the
voyage but to no avail. He now requested that the court
authorise him to repair the ship, sell the ship, then pay
off the repairers and settle the crew's wages.

Reference to Charles Anderson, born 1767, single, the
mate of the ship, who had been engaged in
Newburyport in Juky 1796 to serve as mate for $35 per
month. The crew consisted of 11 men, - the master, the
mate, the second mate, six men and two boys.

AC7/71   **March 2, 1798**

Henderson, Riddel and Company, merchants in
Glasgow, agents and attorneys to Henderson, Ferguson
and Gibson, merchants in Virginia, v. Alexander Stewart
and other merchants in Glasgow, concerning insurance
on the cargo of the American brigantine <u>Catherine</u>,
master Samuel Cazneau, including tobacco from
Virginia and Maryland, bound from the Potomac and the
Patuxent Rivers to Helvoetsluys in the United Provinces
and from there to Rotterdam.

On 17 May 1797 the vessel was captured by a French
privateer the <u>Duguay Frouin</u>, Captain Dulache, and was
taken to Nantz where the cargo was declared to be a
lawful prize on the basis that certain of the ship's

papers were not in order. Cazneau protested to the American Vice-Consul in Nantz on 3 June 1797 that the brigantine <u>Catherine</u> belonged to Anthony and Moses Davenport of Newburyport, Massachusetts, and that all the necessary papers were in order before the ship left Nottingham, Virginia.

AC7/72   **March 2, 1798**

Cornelius Calvert in Virginia, his attorney Captain James Tucker in Norfolk, Virginia, and George Brown & John Lawrie, merchants in Glasgow, v. James McDowal and other merchants in Glasgow. The case concerns the brigantine <u>Betsy and Molly,</u> master Thomas Calvert, which sailed from the Clyde bound for Norfolk, Virginia, on 27 October 1775, which had been insured by the said Glasgow merchants. On 25 January 1776 the ship was captured between Cape Henry, near Norfolk, and Hampton Roads by the <u>Edward</u> a tender, master Richard Bouger, belonging to the British frigate <u>Liverpool</u>, Captain John Bellew. Cornelius Calvert was deprived of his ship by Lord Dunmore. Later the vessel was taken to New York where it was declared to be a prize on 4 March 1778 by Robert Bayard, Judge of the Vice Admiralty Court of New York.

AC7/71   **March 9, 1798**

William Rowe, merchant in Newcastle, Archibald Alves
of Springfield, and Alexander Briggs, merchant in
Dalkeith, v. Robert Scott in Belfast.

AC7/72   **June 15, 1798**

James Jopp, merchant in London, and John Taylor WS,
v. John Scott, farmer in Balbuthie, Colinsburgh, Fife,
and Andrew Scott, shipbuilder in Burntisland, regarding
a bill of exchange signed by John Douglas, master of
the brig <u>Sally of Kirkcaldy</u> at Kingston, Jamaica, on 12
March 1796 and drawn on John McDonnell, merchant in
Dublin.

AC7/71   **June 22, 1798**

John Lafford, shipmaster in Greenock, v. William Lourie,
toolmaker in Potter Row, Edinburgh. Reference to 6
boxes of joiners tools bound for John Allan, merchant in
Charleston, South Carolina, on the <u>Mary</u> from the Clyde
to Charleston on 16 February 1798.

AC7/71   **November 23, 1798**

Perrot Johnson and Company v. Andrew McKenzie,
sometime merchant in Glasgow, afterwards in London,
now in the West Indies.

AC7/73   **December 21, 1798**

Alexander Birtwhistle of Dundeugh v. Archibald
McGowan, merchant in Greenock. The case concerns
the <u>Adventure</u>, master Zachariah Swain, which sailed
from New York on 31 January 1798 with a cargo of flax-
seed etc consigned to Archibald McGowan, but was
cast ashore near Boreland in the parish of Girthon,
Kirkcudbrightshire.

AC7/72   **April 12, 1799**

William Sibbald and Company, merchants in Leith,
owners of the <u>Roselle,</u> master David Gourlay, trading
between Leith and Jamaica, v. Robert McLaren, son of
George McLaren manager of the Fordell Coalworks, and
Robert Yeaman, mariners late of the <u>Roselle</u>.

AC7/70   **November 3, 1799**

William Newton of Newton and Mrs Frances Hay or
Anderson, widow of William Anderson, surgeon in
Edinburgh, v. the heirs of John Campbell jr., merchant in
St Ann's, Jamaica.

AC7/73   **August 1, 1800**

**David Kennedy, mariner in Greenock, and Laurence
Crawford, shipmaster in Irvine, v. Captain Malcolm
Dugald, master of the schooner <u>Matilda</u>. In December
1796 Kennedy went on a voyage from the Clyde to
Demerara then to Martinique then to St Vincent and
from there to Trinidad where he was impressed into the
Royal Navy. Kennedy claims for his unpaid wages.**

INDEX OF NAMES

Adair, John, 62
Adair, Thomas, 116
Adam, James, 104
Adams, John, 72
Addison, James, 83
Addison, John, 49, 67
Affan, Hugh, 80
Ainsworth, John, 10, 11
Aitchison, John, 37
Aitken, James, 57
Aitken, John, 57
Aitken, Robert, 50
Aiton, Andrew, 57
Alexander, Claud, 73
Alexander, David, 24, 26, 27, 28
Alexander, John, 63
Alexander, Robert, 22, 83
Alexander, William, 57
Allan, Alexander, 89, 93
Allan, John, 127
Allan, Richard, 111
Allan, Robert, 34, 35
Allan, William, 82
Alston, Gavin, 114
Alston, John, 80, 116
Alves, Archibald, 127
Alves, Thomas, 39, 41
Alves, ..., 81
Ancrum, Michael, 79
Anderson, Andrew, 8
Anderson, Charles, 125
Anderson, George, 71
Anderson, James, 52
Anderson, John, 4, 62, 63, 64
Anderson, William, 24, 26, 27,
    33, 42, 44, 45, 113

Annand, Katherine, 66
Anson, Leonard, J, 94
Anstruther, Alexander, 10, 20
Apler, Adam, 59
Arbuthnott, Alexander, 30, 31
Armour, James, 1, 3
Armour, John, 45
Armstrong, John, 89
Armstrong, Samuel, 122
Arnott, David, 28
Arnot, Henry, 89
Arrowsmith, Rosella, 27
Arthur, Robert, 16, 17, 18, 55
Arthur, William, 16
Auchenleck, John, 63
Auchenleck, ..., 19
Auchterlony, Alexander, 21
Auchterlony, George, 21
Auld, Robert, 47
Austin, George, 62
Avery, Joseph, 53
Ayton, Andrew, 64
Back, Robert, 93
Backshell, William, 53
Bailey, Robert, 72, 88
Baillie, Alexander, 37, 39, 50
Baillie, Hugh, 39, 50
Baillie, James, 33, 34
Baillie, John, 120, 121
Baird, John, 15, 44, 52, 55, 57
Baird, Robert, 4, 5, 6
Bald, Adam, 28
Balfour, Archibald, 50, 52
Balfour, James, 82
Ballard, Charles, 23
Ballentyne, William, 28
Ballingall, Roger, 77

Banks, David, 52
Baptista, John, 58
Barber, Nathaniel, 97
Barclay, James, 14, 18
Barclay, John, 24
Barclay, Peter, 58
Barnes, Robert, 1
Barro, ..., 108
Barry, Robert, 70
Bartlett, James, 58
Bayard, Robert, 126
Bayne, Kenneth, 8
Beattie, George, 20, 21
Beale, Othnell, 62
Bell, Daniel, 54
Bell, Richard, 64
Bell, William, 78
Bellew, John, 126
Benn, Henry, 28
Benn, Richard, 15
Benn, Robert, 28
Bentley, George, 4, 5
Berry, James, 58
Beveridge, James, 82
Bidles, Elisha, 46
Biggan, John, 121, 122
Bingham, William, 100
Binning, John, 28, 31, 33, 39
Birtwhistle, Alexander, 128
Black, Agnes, 122
Black, Hugh, 22
Black, James, 12
Black, Peter, 74
Blackburn, Andrew, 119, 120
Blackwood, Robert, 10
Blain, ..., 124
Blair, Alexander, 106
Blair, David, 25, 105
Blair, James, 21, 45, 50

Blair, John, 43
Blair, Thomas, 28
Blair, Walter, 30, 38
Blane, John, 44
Blundell, ..., 123
Blundell, Brien, 62
Blyth, William, 52
Bodwin, William, 59
Bog, Robert, 110
Bogle, George, 42, 116
Bogle, James, 1
Bogle, John, 14, 15, 16. 17, 22,
    26, 27, 55
Bogle, Matthew, 65, 66
Bogle, Robert, 15, 36, 38
Bogle, Thomas, 65, 66
Boick, Hugh, 3
Boick, William, 3
Boog, Hugh, 1
Bordeaux, David, 90
Bork, William, 1
Bouger, Richard, 126
Bowdoin, James, 103
Bowman, Jeremiah, 22
Bowman, Samuel, 45
Bowman, William, 39
Boyd, Adam, 44, 45
Boyd, Alexander, 49
Boyd, James, 44, 101
Boyd, John, 39, 40
Boyd, Robert, 78
Boyd, Thomas, 101, 118
Boyle, George, 1
Boyle, James, 2
Boyle, Robert, 1, 38
Boyle, William, 1, 3, 49
Brabner, James, 12
Brakell, John, 62
Brauchill, John, 51

Brewer, Thomas, 27
Briggs, Alexander, 127
Brimmer, Andrew, 103
Brimmer, Herman, 103
Brisk, ..., 18
Brown, George, 126
Brown, Hugh, 121
Brown, James, 8, 83
Brown, Robert, 28, 29
Brown, Thomas, 89
Brown, William, 94
Bruce, Andreas, 7
Bryce, Archibald, 102, 105
Bryce, Ninian, 51
Bryce, William, 51
Bryde, Archibald, 102
Bryon, George, 88
Bryson, Robert, 50, 52
Buchan, Arichibald, 112
Buchan, David, 23
Buchan, Neil, 42
Buchanan, Andrew, 21, 34, 73
Buchanan, Archibald, 55, 99
Buchanan, George, 71, 73, 85, 99
Buchanan, James, 73
Buchanan, John, 23, 38, 43, 48, 85, 99
Buchanan, Neil, 34
Buchanan, Patrick, 22
Bulkeley, Charles, 116
Bull, Robert, 57
Bunteine, Robert, 30, 34, 38, 65
Burden, Robert, 15
Burgers, ..., 10
Burne, William, 24
Burnett, John, 56, 63
Burnet, Robert, 20, 21
Burnet, Thomas, 20, 21

Burton, John, 105
Calbart, Robert, 122
Caddel, Alexander, 113
Calder, Alexander, 93
Calder, John, 22
Calder, Thomas, 47
Calhoun, James, 52
Calhoun, William, 115
Calvert, Cornelius, 126
Calvert, Thomas, 126
Cameron, Daniel, 112
Cameron, John, 57
Campbell, Agnes, 8
Campbell, Alexander, 77, 124
Campbell, Archibald, 64, 109
Campbell, David, 77
Campbell, George, 6
Campbell, Hay, 112, 113
Campbell, Isobel, 107, 108, 119, 120
Campbell, James, 25, 105, 123
Campbell, John, 98, 119, 128
Campbell, Neil, 95, 115
Campbell, Peter, 95
Carkett, James, 1
Carmalt, John, 109
Carmichael, Christopher, 28
Carmichael, John, 71, 72
Carnegie, Thomas, 79
Carnegie, William, 110
Carstairs, Alexander, 27, 28
Carstairs, John, 20
Carter, David Gavin, 27
Cathcart, Andrew, 55, 56
Cathcart, Fergus, 14
Cathcart, Hugh, 56
Cathcart, Robert, 14
Cathe, Gavin, 27
Cattenach, Donald, 82

Cattenach, William, 82
Cazneau, Samuel, 125, 126
Chapland, George, 20, 21
Chapman, Janet, 79
Charnley, Edward, 27
Charters, Charles, 2, 6
Charters, John, 22
Cheap, Patrick, 27
Cheap, Peter, 19
Cheever, John, 93
Chiesley, Samuel, 28, 29
Chinnery, John, 87
Christie, John, 112
Christie, Thomas, 67
Church, Nathan, 101
Clark, Benjamin, 103
Clark, Duncan, 112, 113
Clerk, Hugh, 64
Clark, James, 108, 109
Clerk, John, 18, 35, 47, 65
Clerk, Jonathan, 54, 91
Clark, Robert, 44
Clark, Thomas, 52
Clark, William, 97, 111
Cleghorn, Thomas, 103
Clogess, William, 46
Clyde, David, 122
Coats, Archibald, 64
Coats, John, 64
Coates, Thomas, 26, 32
Cochrane, Andrew, 42
Cochran, David, 87
Cochran, John, 6
Cochrane, Robert, 62
Cockburn, Andrew, 8, 9, 10
Cockburn, Archibald, 54
Cockburn, Martha, 122
Codbert, William, 32
Colman, James, 23

Colquhoun, Laurence, 52
Colyier, William, 12
Cook, Ralph, 107
Cooper, Daniel, 27
Cooper, William, 28
Copland, William, 65
Corbett, James, 2, 18, 47
Corbett, Walter, 43
Cordes, Joseph, 93
Cormack, Robert, 59, 66
Corsan, Adam, 118
Corson, James, 31
Corson, Robert, 31
Coulter, James, 71, 80
Coulter, John, 35, 56, 57
Coulter, Michael, 35
Cowan, Andrew, 64
Cowan, Patrick, 83
Coward, William, 99
Craig, George, 21, 22
Craig, John, 21
Craig, William, 44, 45, 55
Craigie, James, 14
Craigie, Lawrence, 14
Craimare, Thomas, 47
Craine, William, 34
Cranston, Samuel, 24
Crawford, Alexander, 5
Crawford, James, 12, 45, 52, 65,
    84, 102, 105
Crawford, John, 4, 5
Crawford, Laurence, 129
Crawford, Matthew, 44
Crawford, Patrick, 5
Crawford, Robert, 111
Crawford, Samuel, 102, 105
Crawford, Thomas, 4, 15, 78, 87
Crichton, John, 39, 41
Crighton, Alexander, 47

Crockatt, Archibald, 124
Crockatt, Charles, 53
Crockett, James, 52, 53
Crockett, John, 52, 53
Croft, Abraham, 62
Cross, John, 66, 71
Crosver, Robert, 31
Cruso, John, 59
Cumberledge, Christopher, 57
Cumberledge, Elizabeth, 57
Cunningham, Alexander, 78
Cunningham, Janet, 2
Cunningham, John, 35
Cunningham, Peter, 124
Cunningham, William, 43, 44, 76, 91
Currie, George, 23, 42
Curtis, Thomas, 7
Cutler, Edward, 25
Dallas, Thomas, 76
Dalling, James, 25
Dalling, William, 11
Dalrymple, Charles, 14
Dalrymple, John, 60
Daniel, Andrew, 59
Daniel, George, 18
Daniel, John, 24, 28
Dart, John, 62
Davenport, Anthony, 126
Davenport, Moses, 126
Davidson, Alexander, 20, 53, 54
Davidson, ..., 119
Davies, Howell, 18, 19
Davis, Joshua, 1
Davis, William, 2
Daw, Duncan, 19, 24
Dawes, William, 96
Dawling, Isobel, 22
Dawling, James, 22

Dawson, Adam, 113
Dean, Donald, 108
Dean, John, 98
Deas, John, 71
De Newfsville, John, 101
Dennie, James, 22
Denniston, Jaes, 70
Dennistoun, Walter, 10
Dewar, James, 70
Dewsbie, James, 94
Dick, Gilbert, 7
Dick, John, 83
Dickie, Robert, 67
Dickson, John, 28, 29
Dickson, William, 101
Dinning, James, 30
Dinwiddie, Laurence, 57
Dishell, Thomas, 23
Dixon, Jonathan, 101
Doig, Peter, 113
Dolson, Thomas, 114
Donald, James, 98, 101, 104, 114
Donald, Robert, 63, 114
Donald, William, 98, 101
Donaldson, William, 62, 63, 64
Dorsey, Dennis, 95
Dorwall, William, 8
Dougal, John, 64
Douglas, Alexander, 8
Douglas, Hugh, 62
Douglas, Isabel, 89
Douglas, John, 73, 127
Douglas, Robert, 62, 89
Douglas, Thomas, 67
Dowden, Thomas, 18, 67
Drinnan, Robert, 106
Drummond, David, 8
Drummond, Robert, 112
Drummond, William, 10

Drysdale, Alexander, 89
Duff, Alexander, 22
Dugald, Malcolm, 129
Duguid, John, 118
Dulache, ..., 125
Dunbar, Charles, 17, 18
Dunbar, George, 39
Dunbar, James, 22, 39
Dunbar, Robert, 67
Dunbar, William, 77
Duncan, George, 65
Duncan, John, 79, 119, 120, 121
Duncan, Walter, 37
Duncanson, James, 64
Dundas, Alexander, 26, 27, 54
Dundas, Charles, 27
Dundas, Walter, 29
Dundas, William, 49
Dunlop, Archibald, 77
Dunlop, Colin, 73
Dunlop, Hugh, 111
Dunlop, James, 75
Dunlop, John, 43
Dunlop, Robert, 32, 116
Dunlop, William, 7, 43
Dunmore, Robert, 98, 108, 119, 120
Dunmore, Thomas, 77
Dunmore, ..., 127
Dunnet, John, 88
Dunning, James, 31
Dupuy, Michael, 96
Dusin, Codata, 105
Dyce, James, 65
Dyce, Janet, 65
Dykes, John, 88
Easdale, John, 44
Eason, Robert, 106, 107
Eccles, William, 16

Edgar, John, 24
Edgar, Joseph, 12
Edgar, Thomas, 24
Edie, Donald, 78
Edmonstone, Archibald, 52
Egglesfield, George, 22
Elliot, Cornelius, 78
Elliot, David, 115
Elphinstone, John, 71
Elston, John, 89
Eshwell, John, 18
Evans, Nicolas, 23
Ewing, Walter, 116
Fairholm, Adam, 73
Fairnie, Alexander, 111
Fall, William, 35, 41
Fallafield, Isaac, 8
Farley, William, 110, 113
Farming, Thomas, 105
Farris, William, 92
Fenton, William, 18
Ferguson, David, 8
Ferguson, James, 50
Ferguson, Hugh, 33
Ferguson, Robert, 87, 113
Fettes, William, 109
Finlay, George, 109
Findlay, James, 118
Finlayson, John, 13
Finlayson, Robert, 64
Fisher, Walter, 113
Fleming, Gardner, 75
Fleming, George, 100
Fleming, John, 112
Fleming, Thomas, 30, 34, 37
Fleming, William, 115
Fletcher, John, 22, 90
Flint, James, 62
Flows, Roger, 23

Houstoun, Patrick, 51
Howard, Michael, 22
Howatt, James, 1, 3
Hows, Roger, 18, 26
Humbley, Clem, 27
Hunter, Charles, 95, 107
Hunter, David, 79
Hunter, James, 52, 60, 114
Hunter, Matthew, 83
Hunter, Patrick, 114
Hunter, William, 39, 41, 75
Hutchison, John, 39
Hutton, Alexander, 23
Hutton, James, 77, 178
Hyndman, Archibald, 43
Huslop, James, 107
Inch, Jean, 53
Inglis, Alexander, 12
Inglis, James, 81
Inglis, John, 117
Inglis, Patrick, 25
Inglis, Samuel, 100
Ingram, Archibald, 71
Innes, George, 90
Innes, John, 12
Jack, Andrew, 116
Jackson, Joseph, 22
Jackson, Robert, 21
Jacobsen, Herman, 101
Jagart, Abraham, 3
Jagart, Francis, 3
Jamieson, Alexander, 56
Jamison, John, 10, 55
Jameson, Patrick, 13
Jarret, John, 18
Jerbie, John, 22
Johnson, Perrot, 127
Johnston, David, 89
Johnston, Duncan, 112

Johnstone, James, 71, 73
Johnston, John, 3
Johnston, Mathew, 106
Johnston, Thomas, 109
Jones, Edward, 57
Jones, John, 23
Jones, John Coffin, 97
Jones, Philip, 27
Jones, Richard, 18
Jones, Thomas, 120, 121
Jones, William, 57
Jophen, Dennis, 18
Jopp, James, 127
Justine, John, 1
Keith, Robert, 10
Kemp, Gavin, 109
Kennedy, Alexander, 79
Kennedy, David, 10, 129
Kennedy, Hugh, 33
Kennedy, John, 79
Kennedy, Oliver, 24
Kennedy, ..., 19
Keppie, George, 66
Kerny, Nicolas, 18
Kerr, Alexander, 121
Kerr, John, 1, 38
Kerr, Margaret, 113
Kerr, Robert, 106, 107
Kilpatrick, J., 43
King, John, 37, 39, 43, 48, 52
Kinloch, John, 47
Kippen, John, 96, 97
Kirkcaldy, David, 107
Kitchen, Daniel, 22
Knight, James, 7
Knight, Thomas, 43
Knox, Thomas, 63, 64
Kyle, John, 10
Laing, John, 49, 55

Lafford, John, 127
Lampo, Samuel, 67
Land, John, 117
Lander, David, 8
Lang, Gabriel, 110
Langtoun, Isaack, 26
Laudenberg, George, 59
Laurie, Gavin, 80
Laverock, John, 82, 83, 114
Lawrie, John, 126
Lawson, Peter, 91
Leary, John, 100
Lee, Joseph, 97
Lee, Robert, 96
Leider, Thomas, 3
Leitch, Andrew, 16
Lewis, John, 99
Lewis, Matthew, 91
Lewis, William, 30, 32, 91
Liddel, James, 24
Liddell, Duncan, 117
Liddelll, Robert, 116
Lindsay, Alexander, 42
Lindquist, John, 80
Loch, David, 76, 78
Lockhart, Thomas, 10
Lockhart, William, 6
Logan, George, 108, 119, 120
Longhead, David, 50
Longmuir, John, 114
Lord, Samuel, 97
Lourie, William, 127
Love, Alexander, 120, 121
Lowdon, William, 106
Lowe, William, 31
Lowis, Edward, 39, 42
Lowis, Elizabeth, 39
Ludat, Thomas, 33
Luke, John, 42, 57

Lumsden, John, 56
Luntly, Richard, 18
Lush, Hannibal, 109
Lutewadge, Thomas, 23, 31, 42, 43
Lyon, George, 4, 5, 6, 7, 33
Lyon, James, 117
Lyon, John, 38, 72, 113
McBrayer, James, 22
McBride, Hugh, 50
McCallum, Archibald, 110
McCathie, Peter, 53
McCaul, Alexander, 119, 120
McCaull, George, 102, 105, 114
McCaull, Henry, 39, 42, 47
McCaull, Samuel, 13, 32, 36, 38
McCaustelin, Duncan, 47
McCaver, James, 35
McChiere, Antony, 27
McChiere, William, 27
McCloster, Joseph, 23
McCormack, Edward, 34
McCou, Samuel, 22
McCree, William, 79
McCulloch, Alexander, 25
McCulloch, George, 109
McCulloch, James, 34, 35
McCurly, Alexander, 111
McDonald, George, 82
McDonald, William, 82, 83
McDonnell, John, 127
McDougall, Alexander, 72, 89
McDougall, Patrick, 8
McDowall, James, 111, 126
McFarland, John, 21
McFarlane, Alexander, 60
McFarlane, John, 21, 39, 40, 42
McFarlane, William, 72
McFie, James Tulloch, 79
McGibbon, James, 77

McGowan, Archibald, 128
McGowan, Robert, 45
McHattie, Peter, 58
McIlraith, Andrew, 24
McIntosh, Alexander, 22
McIntosh, ..., 19
McIver, John, 110
Mackay, Alexander, 82, 83
McKay, Allan, 93
McKay, Daniel, 47, 48
MacKay, Duff, 48
McKay, Tim, 58
McKay, William, 41, 48
McKenna, John, 72, 88, 89
McKenzie, Andrew, 115, 127
McKenzie, George, 53
McKenzie, James, 72
McKenzie, John, 25, 60
McKenzie, Kenneth, 53
McKenzie, Roderick, 9, 11
McKenzie, William, 60
McKinlay, Allan, 92, 93
McKinnon, James, 84
McKinnon, John, 83
McKirdy, Robert, 97
McKnight, William, 40
McLaren, George, 128
McLaren, Robert, 128
McLarty, Archibald, 79
McLauchlan, Hugh, 70
McLean, James, 91
McLean, John, 54, 79
McLellan, Dougal, 94
McMichan, Gilbert, 15
McNair, James, 22, 67, 71
McNair, Robert, 67, 71
McNeill, Archibald, 123
McNeil, John, 116
McReadie, ..., 50

McReith, Samuel, 3
McRennet, Hugh, 46
McRob, Duncan, 109
McSpedden, James, 122
McTaggart, William, 10
Machell, Willis, 100, 101, 103
Madder, John, 10
Maddocks, William, 58
Mansfield, James, 71
Margetson, James, 103, 104
Margetson, John, 99, 100, 101
Marshall, Andrew, 89
Mason, Jonathon, 103
Mason, John, 22
Mason, William, 22
Massey, Nicolas, 105
Mathison, George, 52
Matthewson, Thomas, 15
Maxwell, Colin, 113
Maxwell, James, 113
Maxwell, John, 10
Maxwell, ..., 27
Mears, James, 35
Melville, James, 35
Menzies, Charles, 16
Menzies, Robert, 70
Menzies, ..., 20
Michie, James, 72
Middleton, Alexander, 52
Miller, Charles, 33, 34
Miller, James, 10, 57, 82, 86
Miller, John, 16
Miller, Robert, 98
Miller, Thomas, 34
Miller, William, 58, 84, 86
Milliken, Hugh, 63
Minty, William, 18
Minors, John, 8
Minors, Robert, 8

Mitchell, David, 24
Mitchell, Janet, 23
Mitchell, John, 21
Mitchell, Patrick, 82
Mitchell, Thomas, 65, 66
Mitchell, William, 102, 109
Moncrieff, George, 52, 66
Montford, Joseph, 80
Montgomery, James, 78, 87
Montgomery, John, 122, 123
Montgomery, Peter, 47
Montgomery, Walter, 45, 65
Montier, James, 47, 50
Monteith, Walter, 87
Moor, John, 16
Moore, Roger, 72
More, Gilbert, 10
Morgan, George, 82
Morris, James, 94
Morris, Robert, 100
Morrison, Alexander, 65
Morrison, Donald, 115
Morrison, James, 84
Morrison, John, 71
Morrison, Robert, 100
Morrison, William, 94, 113
Mossman, George, 11
Mowbray, John, 14
Munro, Andrew, 48
Munro, John, 85, 87, 89, 93, 97,
    99, 100, 101, 102, 103, 113
Munro, Joseph, 101
Murchie, Archibald, 47
Murchy, John, 114
Murdoch, John, 32
Murdoch, Peter, 52
Mure, John, 15
Murieson, James, 14
Murphy, Matthew, 47

Murray, Alexander, 1
Murray, John, 1
Murray, Thomas, 72
Murray, William, 78
Napier, William, 1, 3
Neall, John, 78
Needs, Thomas, 46
Neilson, James, 63
Newall, Abraham, 96
Newall, Abraham, 96, 122
Newhame, Roger, 3
Newman, Thomas, 85, 86
Newton, William, 128
Nicholson, Clement, 23, 33, 34, 42
Nicholson, John, 34
Nicol, George, 82
Nicoll, William, 54
Nisbet, Alexander, 62
Nisbet, James, 19
Niven, John, 46
Noble, William, 30, 78
Noyes, David, 86
Ogilvy, Alexander, 92, 107
Ogilvie, James, 76
Ord, George, 100
Orrock, Walter, 69
Orry, ..., 93
Oswald, Alexander, 54, 55, 62
Oswald, Richard, 54, 62
Pagan, David, 114
Pain, William, 58
Park, Arthur, 15, 28
Parker, Paul, 34
Partis, Matthias, 9
Partridge, Richard, 24
Partridge, Robert, 24
Paterson, David, 109, 123
Paterson, Hugh, 83, 123
Paterson, James, 118

Paterson, John, 76, 113
Paterson, Peter, 75, 76
Paterson, Solomon, 30
Paterson, William, 28
Peacock, Robert, 114
Peadie, James, 16
Pearson, Joseph, 15
Pearsting, Richard, 25
Peel, John, 34
Penman, James, 108
Perkins, John, 58
Petrie, David, 23
Petrie, William, 56
Pettigrew, William, 29, 32
Philips, ..., 2
Pillan, Mary, 122
Plenderleith, David, 8
Polling, Mary, 122
Pollock, Duncan, 73
Pollock, Robert, 10
Porter, James, 42
Porter, John W., 123
Porter, ..., 18
Potts, William, 80
Power, Richard, 30, 31
Price, John, 69
Pringle, Robert, 25
Quarrel, William Dawes, 98
Rae, Robert, 45, 63, 65
Rae, Thomas, 65
Rae, William, 12
Ramage, Alexander, 81, 82
Ramsay, Andrew, 30, 42
Ramsay, Charles, 20, 21
Ramsay, Thomas, 84
Rathbon, Patrick, 104
Reid, Alexander, 6
Reid, James, 84, 85, 86
Reid, Thomas, 91

Reid, William, 46
Reynolds, John, 10
Riddell, John, 38, 119, 120
Rigg, John, 52
Ritchie, Alexander, 75, 122
Ritchie, Daniel, 105
Ritchie, Dougal, 115
Ritchie, George, 57
Ritchie, James, 116
Robb, Agnes, 3
Robb, Ann, 113
Robb, Elizabeth, 113
Robb, Isobel, 113
Robb, James, 113
Robb, Janet, 113
Robb, Patrick, 113
Robb, William, 113
Roberts, ..., 19, 104
Robertson, Archibald, 117
Robertson, Charles, 40
Robertson, David, 41, 83
Robertson, George, 119
Robertson, James, 8, 22
Robertson, John, 23, 41, 47
Robertson, Matthew, 49, 55
Robertson, Robert, 24, 26, 32, 38,
    117
Robertson, William, 28, 29, 113
Rodger, Hugh, 52
Roger, George, 22
Roger, Thomas, 18
Ronald, George, 52
Ronalds, Hugh, 35
Ronaldson, Andrew, 78
Ross, Andrew, 53
Ross, Charles, 85
Ross, David, 85
Ross, George, 93
Ross, Hugh, 85

Ross, James, 65
Ross, John, 77, 192, 108, 111
Ross, William, 60
Ross, ..., 91
Rowan, Stephen, 85
Rowand, John, 69, 70
Rowe, William, 127
Russell, Francis, 98, 101, 104, 105
Russell, Jean, 75
Russell, Samuel, 15
Rutherford, David
Ruthven, Patricia, 8
Ryburn, James, 112
Rymer, Mary, 8
Rymond, Richard, 30, 31
St John, Barnet, 27
Sangster, John, 47
Sarrate, ..., 80
Saturley, Hayman, 18
Saul, James, 18
Schaw, John, 10
Scott, Andrew, 127
Scott, George, 15
Scott, James, 51, 95
Scott, John, 127
Scott, Oliver, 66
Scott, Robert, 47, 64, 115, 127
Scott, Thomas, 80
Scott, Walter, 73, 88
Scuton, George, 80
Seaman, George, 52, 71, 72
Seaman, James, 53, 71
Seaman, John, 52
Sears, Isaac, 101
Seaton, George, 10
Sextroh, William, 89, 90
Shearer, William, 27
Sheddan, John, 107
Sheever, John, 93

Shepherd, John, 12
Sherwine, Robert, 15
Shiells, John, 121
Shortridge, John, 80
Sibbald, Alexander, 95
Simpson, John, 98, 104
Sinclair, Gustavus, 50, 52
Skene, Alexander, 37, 39
Skene, George, 37, 39
Skene, Samuel, 122
Skinner, Thomas, 100
Skirving, Katherine, 66
Sloan, John, 106
Smith, Abraham, 62
Smith, Archibald, 95
Smith, Benjamin, 62
Smith, Bernard, 43
Smith, Duncan, 117
Smith, James, 67
Smith, John, 34, 87, 112
Smith, Samuel, 69
Smith, Thomas, 13, 69
Smith, William, 10, 99
Smithson, Thomas, 34
Smollet, Christopher, 103
Snodgrass, John, 102, 103, 105
Snodgrass, William, 102, 105
Soderstrom, Charles, 100
Somerville, John, 51
Spencer, Harry, 30, 31, 32
Spense, Thomas, 10
Spotswood, Alexander, 16
Spreull, David, 33
Spreull, James, 42, 71
Squire, Matthew, 85
Stark, John, 44, 45, 46, 47. 48, 49
Steel, Robert, 22
Steers, Joseph, 88
Stein, Janet, 107

Stein, John, 107
Stenhouse, John, 28
Stevenson, Alexander, 10
Stewart, Alexander, 125
Stewart, Andrew, 69
Stewart, Archibald, 62
Stewart, James, 72, 108
Stewart, John, 10, 54, 66, 122
Stewart, Peter, 113
Stewart, Robert, 7, 11, 93, 123
Stewart, Roger, 123
Stewart, William, 122
Stirling, John, 33
Stock, Humphrey, 58
Stocks, Ebenezer, 96
Stone, Zachariah, 52
Stott, ..., 119
Strachan, Robert, 23
Strain, David, 122
Straton, Henry, 20, 21
Strong, Soloman, 80
Strummely, John, 100
Swain, Zachariah, 128
Swordly, John, 50
Syme, Isabel, 106
Symms, John, 46
Tait, James, 121, 122
Tait, William, 73
Tawse, John, 83
Taylor, Alexander, 94, 96, 99
Taylor, Archibald, 50
Taylor, James, 84
Taylor, John, 45, 65, 127
Taylor, Samuel, 45
Temple, James, 108
Tennant, John, 75, 76
Thixton, Henry, 18
Thomson, Alexander, 52, 54
Thomson, Andrew, 102, 105

Thomson, David, 112
Thomson, Duncan, 84
Thomson, George, 42
Thompson, James, 31
Thomson, John, 54
Thomson, Robert, 23
Thomson, Thomas, 36, 107
Thomson, William, 10, 96
Thurston, Edward, 24, 25
Titcomb, Jonathan, 124, 125
Tod, Archibald, 74
Tod, Charles, 74
Tod, George, 45, 65
Tod, John, 13, 74
Tod, Oliver, 74
Tod, Richard, 74
Tod, Robert, 62, 63, 64, 74
Tod, William, 74
Tolmie, Alexander, 22, 42
Tolmie, David, 41
Topps, Joseph, 46
Tran, Arthur, 16, 18, 26, 32, 36,
    38, 51
Trotter, John, 70, 89
Troup, William, 8
Tubman, Edward, 35
Tuck, William, 52
Tucker, James, 126
Tucker, Joseph, 15
Tufts, John, 103
Tullideph, Walter, 70
Turberville, George, 55
Turnbull, George, 9
Turnbull, John, 9
Turner, Daniel, 104
Urquhart, George, 58
Urquhart, Patrick, 58
Urquhart, ..., 53
Vandervolt, John, 90

Vans, Hugh, 46, 47, 48, 49, 52, 60
Verner, Robert, 4
Viccary, John, 93
Wair, John, 23
Walk, Andrew, 49
Walker, Antony, 22
Walker, John, 23
Walker, Nathaniel, 28
Walker, Thomas, 30, 43
Walker, William, 113
Wall, Christopher, 33
Wallace, Ann, 107
Wallace, James, 28, 91
Wallace, John, 24
Wallace, Michael, 13, 118
Wallace, Thomas, 35, 44
Wanton, Phillip, 24
Wanton, William, 24, 25
Warden, William, 44
Wardrop, James, 85
Wardrop, John, 63, 112
Wardrope, Ralph, 112
Wardroper, James, 5
Warrender, Thomas, 10
Watson, Alexander, 16
Watson, Andrew, 109
Watson, James, 17, 18, 54, 62, 63
Watson, John, 10, 28
Watson, Samuel, 89, 114
Watt, James, 57, 60
Wauchope, Henry, 70
Weir, George, 22
Weir, James, 54, 55
Weir, William, 112
Welsh, John, 79
Welch, Samuel, 47, 50, 52
Wemyss, William, 72
Weston, Samuel, 49
Wharrey, James, 42, 48

Whyte, Archibald, 112, 113
White, Bernard, 58
Whyte, David, 8
White, Harry, 23
Whyte, Henry, 88
White, John, 45, 65
Whyte, Thomas, 9
Whitehead, George, 107
Whitelaw, James, 64
Whyteside, Antony, 14, 15, 16
Whiteside, William, 15, 16, 17
Wightman, Charles, 95
Wightman, William, 8
Wilkie, James, 112
Wilkie, Thomas, 112
Willing, Thomas, 100
Wilson, Christopher, 108
Wilson, John, 34
Wilson, Nathan, 124
Wilson, William, 8, 59, 66, 106
Wolsey, John, 9
Wood, David, 89
Woods, James, 115
Wood, John, 73
Woodrow, John, 42
Worsley, Samuel, 45
Worstenholme, Thomas, 62
Wyber, Isaac, 22
Yelton, Thomas, 107
Yeoman, Robert, 128
Yeomans, William, 62
Young, David, 54, 55, 58
Young, Gavin, 124
Young, James, 60
Young, Peter, 58
Young, ..., 15
Yuille, Archibald, 29, 32, 46, 47, 48, 49
Yuille, Thomas, 39, 42

INDEX OF PLACES

49, 55, 83

Aberdeen, Scotland, 12, 39, 56, 60, 63, 65, 71, 125
Accomack County, Virginia, 45
Africa, 67
Airth, Stirlingshire, Scotland, 64, 83
America, 67, 74, 78, 95, 106, 110, 111, 116
Amsterdam, 13, 27, 73, 101, 103, 104
Annanbao, Africa, 19
Antigua, W.I., 13, 16, 17, 18, 19, 46, 69, 70, 71, 77, 109, 110, 111, 112, 118, 123
Ardeer, Ayrshire, Scotland, 98
Ayr, Scotland, 9, 46, 50, 75, 79, 87, 115, 118
Baltimore, Maryland, 99, 117
Bance Island, Africa, 19
Banff, Scotland, 58
Barbados, WI, 14, 19, 23, 25, 26, 27, 28, 29, 34, 35, 36, 37, 40, 46, 48, 64, 67, 71
Barren Island, Chesapeake Bay, 60
Basseterre, St Kitts, WI, 36
Bay of Biscay, 92
Bay of Honduras, 82, 83, 85, 89, 114
Bear Creek, Baltimore County, Maryland, 99
Belfast, Ireland, 28, 34, 35, 121, 127
Bermuda, 67
Bilbao, Portugal, 49
Bo'ness, Scotland, 11, 13, 19, 24,

Bordeaux, France, 73, 92, 97
Boston, Massachusetts, 31, 46, 47, 48, 49, 50, 52, 54, 56, 60, 65, 66, 69, 84, 86, 93, 94, 98, 101, 102, 103, 104
Brazil, 19
Bridgetown, Barbados, 27
Bristol, England, 1, 69
Broadsound, Shetland, 7
Burntisland, Fife, Scotland, 15, 127
Cadiz, Spain, 93
Caithness, Scotland, 81
Calabar, Africa, 36, 37
Campbeltown, Argyll, Scotland, 124
Cape Cod, New England, 93
Cape Fear, North Carolina, 80
Cape Franbaway, Hispaniola, 18
Cape Hatteras, North Carolina, 120, 121
Cape Henloopen, Delaware, 88
Cape Henry, Virginia, 128
Cape Nicola Mole, 120
Capes of Virginia, 85
Carolina, 4, 6, 7, 58, 59, 61, 66, 70, 72, 88
Carthagena, South America, 11, 60
Casco Bay, New England, 92

Charleston, South Carolina, 4, 52, 53, 61, 62, 78, 88, 90, 118, 121, 127

Charlottetown, Prince Edward Island, 106

Clyde River, Scotland, 36, 51, 82, 88, 93, 97, 109, 110, 111, 115, 129

County Antrim, Ireland, 122

County Down, Ireland, 122

County Monaghan, Ireland, 122

Crawforddyke, Scotland, 16, 17, 18, 22, 29, 32, 47, 55, 119

Cromarty, Scotland, 49, 54, 55

Cuba, WI, 18

Cumberland, England, 9, 15, 21, 67

Cumnock, Ayrshire, Scotland, 115

Curacao, WI, 18, 24

Dalkeith, Midlothian, Scotland, 127

Danzig, 56

Delaware River, Delaware, 88

Demerara, South America, 129

Dominica, WI, 115, 119

Dublin, Ireland, 31, 80, 127

Dumfries, Scotland, 106

Dunbar, East Lothian, Scotland, 35, 41, 46

Dundee, Scotland, 10, 63

Duns, Berwickshire, Scotland, 42

Dysart, Fife, Scotland, 114

Ebing, Wurtemburg, Scotland, 59

Edenton, North Carolina, 120, 121

Edinburgh, Scotland, 1, 2, 6, 8, 9, 10, 12, 18, 19, 21, 24, 25, 28, 33, 35, 47, 49, 52, 53, 54, 55, 58, 59, 61, 62, 64, 69, 71, 73, 74, 75, 77, 78, 79, 88, 89, 95, 102, 109, 121, 123, 124, 127

England, 3, 117

Falkirk, Stirlingshire, Scotland, 109

Fisherow, Edinburgh, 66

Fort William, Inverness -shire, Scotland, 55

France, 76, 87, 92, 94, 96

Fraserburgh, Aberdeenshire, Scotland, 58, 101

Glasgow, Scotland, 1, 3, 4, 6, 13, 14, 15, 16, 17, 18, 22, 23, 26, 27, 29, 30, 32, 34, 35, 36, 37, 39, 40, 42, 43, 44, 45, 46, 47, 48, 51, 52, 5, 55, 56, 61, 62, 63, 64, 65, 66, 67, 69, 70, 71, 72, 73, 77, 79, 80, 82, 84, 86, 87, 92, 95, 98, 102, 105, 107, 111, 112, 114, 115, 116, 117, 118, 119, 120, 122, 123, 124

Goochland, Virginia, 103, 105

Gothenborg, Sweden, 90, 100

Gourock, Scotland, 22

Grande Terre, Guadaloupe, WI, 123

Greenock, Scotland, 13, 15, 16, 28, 30, 34, 38, 44, 45, 55, 60, 62, 63, 65, 79, 81, 84, 85, 86, 90, 92, 96, 97, 98, 99, 102, 104, 105, 106,

109, 110, 111, 112,
113, 114, 115, 116,
117, 118, 119, 122,
123, 124, 127, 128,
129

Grenada, WI, 105, 106

Guadaloupe, WI, 96, 122

Guernsey, Channel Islands, 112

Gulf of Florida, 104

Guinea, Africa, 19, 24, 26, 27, 36,
   67, 80

Halifax, Nova Scotia, 106, 110,
   118

Hamburg, Germany, 46, 55

Hampton, Virginia, 108, 114, 126

Harr parish, Virginia, 1

Hanover, Jamaica, 98

Havana, Cuba, 43, 76

Havre de Grace, France, 116

Helvoetsluys, United Provinces,
   125

Hispaniola, WI, 18, 120

Holland, 7, 117

Honduras, 82, 123

Hull, England, 118, 125

Huntly, Aberdeenshire, Scotland,
   56

Inverness, Scotland, 22, 25, 29, 39,
   41, 48, 54, 108

Ipswich, Massachusetts, 85, 86

Ireland, 9, 41, 43, 111, 121

Irvine, Ayrshire, Scotland, 40, 41,
   66, 129

Island Harbor, Antigua, WI, 110

Isle of Man, G.B., 67

Isle of May, WI, 18

Isle of Providence, WI, 18

Jamaica, 12, 20, 21, 24, 29, 43, 44,
   45, 49, 60, 71, 85, 89, 91,

104, 107, 112, 115,
116,117, 119, 121,
124, 128

James County, Virginia, 10

James River, Virginia, 73

Killaley, Ireland, 1

Kilmarnock, Scotland, 75,
   111

Kilwinning, Scotland, 50

Kincardine, Scotland, 107

Kingston, Jamaica, 21, 60,
   70, 74, 79, 117, 127

Kirkcudbright, Scotland,
   106, 128

Leith, Scotland, 3, 7, 11,
   15, 19, 23, 24,
   50, 51, 52, 54, 56,
   58, 59, 61, 62, 66, 70,
   72, 74, 76, 77, 81, 83,
   88, 92, 99, 101, 103,
   107, 109, 123, 128,

Lisbon, Portugal, 46

Liverpool, England, 19, 27,
   62, 80, 116

Liverpool, Nova Scotia, 117

Loch Broom, Scotland, 102,
   108

Loch Ryan, Scotland, 48,
   121

Lochindale, Islay, Scotland,
   92

London, England, 2, 3, 7,
   10, 15, 20, 21, 22,
   24, 53, 54, 58, 59, 77,
   78, 83, 98, 99, 100,
   101, 124, 129

Madeira, 46, 76

Marblehead, New England,
   97

Marstrand, Sweden, 100
Martinique, WI, 73, 110, 129
Maryland, 8, 11, 14, 23, 26, 28, 30,
    32, 38, 45, 49, 55, 56, 60,
    63, 65, 70, 81, 92, 125
Massachusetts, 24, 60, 96, 97, 101
Methil, Fife, Scotland, 69
Mississippi River, 104
Mobile, West Florida, 98, 104
Montrose, Angus, Scotland, 21, 67
Moray Firth, Scotland, 36, 39
Musselburgh, Scotland, 76
Nantes, France, 92, 99, 125, 126
Nantucket, New England, 86
Netherlands, 118
Nevis, WI, 36
New Bristol, New England, 25
New England, 2, 18, 46, 48, 49,
    50, 51, 56, 65, 69, 74, 92
New London, Connecticut, 116
New Providence, Bahamas, 75
New York, 18, 76, 83, 90, 92, 94,
    105, 106, 112, 113, 118,
    124, 126, 128
Newark, Glasgow, Scotland, 3
Newbury, New England, 90, 93,
    96, 97, 101, 125, 126
Newcastle, England, 127
Newfoundland, 118
Newport, Rhode Island, 24, 25
Norfolk, Virginia, 64, 77, 108, 119,
    120, 126
North Carolina, 60, 81, 82, 86, 120
North Faro, 102, 109
Northumberland, England, 42
Norway, 14, 55
Nottingham, Virginia, 120
Nova Scotia, 102, 106, 108, 118
Occacock, North Carolina, 120

Orkney Islands, Scotland, 63
Ostend, Flanders, 19
Oxford, Virginia, 114
Petersburg, Virginia, 108, 119, 120
Philadelphia, Pennsylvania, 18, 46,
    59, 87, 101, 122, 125
Pictou, Nova Scotia, 106
Piscataqua, New Hampshire, 97
Port Louise, WI, 76
Port Royal, Jamaica, 12, 24, 25,
    104
Port Royal, South Carolina, 7
Portsmouth, New Hampshire, 97
Prestonpans, Scotland, 1
Prince Edward Island, 106
Privateer Bay, 18
Pungataigue Creek, Virginia, 45
Quantico, Virginia, 45
Quebec, 107
Queensferry, Scotland, 22, 25
Rappachannick River, Virginia, 16
Rappahannock River, Virginia, 118
Rhode Island, 24
Richmond, Virginia, 105, 106
River Gambia, Africa, 19
River Patuxent, Maryland, 125
River Potomac, Maryland, 31, 33,
    45, 54, 125
River Sarafras, Maryland, 63
River Sorralou, Africa, 19
Rotterdam, Holland, 28, 34, 39, 49,
    59, 117, 125
St Ann's, Jamaica, 128
St Augustine, Florida, 108
St Croix, WI, 76, 102, 109
St Eustatia, WI, 118
St George's, Grenada, 105
St Domingo, WI, 96
St Kitts, WI, 36, 37, 73, 75, 98,

106, 111, 118
St Lucia, WI, 123
St Martins, WI, 97, 111
St Thomas, WI, 119
St Thomas, Jamaica, 72
St Vincent, WI, 129
Saltcoats, Ayrshire, Scotland, 48
Savannah, Georgia, 85
Shetland Islands, Scotland, 7, 81,
    82, 100, 103
Smithfield, Virginia, 85
Somerset County, Virginia, 23
South Carolina, 38, 53, 61, 71, 72,
    122
Spain, 43
Stirling, Scotland, 22, 106, 107
Straits, Gibralter, 39
Stromness, Scotland, 63, 81, 82
Sweden, 13, 56, 100
Tain, Scotland, 85
Thurso, Caithness, Scotland, 81
Tilling Bay, 116
Tiver Town, Massachusetts, 24
Tobago, WI, 95, 108, 124
Torrisdale, Sutherland, Scotland,
    102, 109
Tortula, WI, 109, 122, 123
Trinidad, WI, 129
United States, 91
Veritbay, 107
Virginia, 1, 3, 7, 10, 13, 14, 15, 16,
    22, 23, 24, 25, 26, 27, 28,
        29, 30, 31, 32, 33,
        34, 35, 36, 37, 38, 39,
        40, 41, 42, 43, 45, 46,
        47, 48, 50, 51, 55, 58,
        60, 62, 63, 64, 65, 66,
        67, 70, 71, 74, 75, 79,
        80, 81, 82, 83, 85, 87,

102, 108, 114, 115,
    116, 117, 119, 124,
    125, 127
Waterford, Ireland, 119
West Indies, 4, 9, 12, 19, 20,
    21, 23, 27, 36, 43,
    56, 67, 69, 76, 98,
    109
Whitehaven, England, 13,
    14, 15, 21, 22, 23,
    26, 28, 30, 31, 32, 34,
    42
Williamsburg, Virginia, 17
Wilmington, North Carolina,
    81, 84, 86
Wurtemberg, Germany, 59
York River, Virginia, 67
Yorkshire, England, 67
Youghal, Ireland, 43

INDEX OF SHIPS

Adventure, 70, 128
Adventure of Whitehaven, 34
Africa, 95
Agatha, 108
Agnes, 75
Ajax, 98, 99
Albany, 28, 29
Alexander, 52
America, 51
America of Glasgow, 43
American Planter of Leith, 82
Amity, 12
Amity of Whitehaven, 34
Anne, 115
Anne galley, 66
Ann of Edinburgh, 50, 52
Ann galley of Inverness, 22, 24
Anna of Glasgow, 14
Annabella of Greenock, 62, 64
Annabella of Saltcoats, 63
Armisted of New York, 124
Bachelor of Leith, 81, 82
Baltimore of Glasgow, 56
Beattie of Bo'ness, 13
Becky and Harriat of Boston, 101, 104
Benjamin of Honduras, 83, 89, 114
Betsy, 85, 86, 108
Betsy and Molly, 126
Betty, 51
Betty of Glasgow, 44, 119
Beverley of Glasgow, 82
Bon Accord of Aberdeen, 60
Brisbane, 29, 32, 46, 48
Brisbane of Port Glasgow, 45, 47
Britannia, 80

Brotherhood of Whitehaven, 22
Burk, 18
Caledonia, 66, 93
Carolina, 79, 80
Carolina Merchant, 7
Castle Semple, 111
Cathcart, 65
Cathcart of Glasgow, 44
Cathcart of Greenock, 30, 34, 38, 45
Catherine, 125, 126
Catherine of Whitehaven, 28
Centurion of Whitehaven, 13, 39
Ceres, 106
Chance of Greenock, 98, 100, 102, 103
Charlotte of Philadelphia, 93
Charming Rachel of London, 58
Christian, 83
Christian of Leith, 23
Commander, 109
Confirmation of Workington, 21, 22
Cumberland, 52
Cupid, 104
Daphne, 88
Diamond of Glasgow, 54, 55
Diligence of Aberdeen, 65
Diligence of Glasgow, 33
Dolphin, 11
Drummond of Glasgow, 29
Dublin, 118
Duguay Frouin, 125
Eagle, 18
Eagle of New York, 19, 26
Eclipse of Baltimore, 92
Edinburgh, 78, 79

Edward, 126
Edward and Sarah of Barbados, 19
Elephant, 94
Elizabeth of Greenock, 124
Elizabeth of London, 63
Elizabeth of Montrose, 20, 21
Elizabeth of Philadelphia, 87, 88
Elizabeth and Mary of London, 3
Elizabeth and Peggy of Leith,73,
      88
Elizabeth and Thomas, 117
Endeavour, 110
Endeavour of Glasgow, 96
Endeavour of Weymouth, 7
Euphan, 13
Euphemia, 61
Fanny of Greenock, 117,118
Favour of Whitehaven, 43
Fortune of Glasgow, 16, 17, 18
Four Friends of Glasgow, 103
Friendship, 64, 109, 110, 118
Friendship of Ayr, 57, 87
Friendship of Leith, 11
Friendship of Rhode Island, 25
Glencairn, 118
Globe of Whitehaven, 25
Greenock of Glasgow, 34
Greenwich, 104
Guernsey Lilly of London, 56
Gustavus of Philadelphia, 100
Hanna, 115
Hannah, 112
Hannah galley, 10
Hannah of Liverpool, 62
Hannah of Rotterdam, 59
Hanover of Glasgow, 36, 38
Hanover of Irvine, 40, 41
Happy Return of Port Glasgow, 43
Hawke of Greenock, 96, 97

Helen, 71
Helen of Leith, 71, 78
Hero, 94
HMS Africa, 107
HMS Daphne, 87
HMS Enterprize, 110
HMS Leopard, 43
HMS Liverpool, 126
HMS Mermaid, 12
HMS Otter, 85
HMS Ramillies, 116
HMS Somerset, 93
Hope, 53, 58
Hope of Bo'ness, 49
Hopewell, 8, 123
Hound, 104
Hunter, 87
Industry, 64, 116
Integrity of Whitehaven, 28
James, 35
James of Dundee, 62
Jean, 29, 32, 45, 68, 71
Jean of Greenock, 44
Jenny, 91
Jessie, 115
John, 95, 119, 120
Joanna of Glasgow, 73
John of Irvine, 40
John of Leith, 92
John of London, 3, 52
John of Portsmouth, New
      Hampshire, 54
John and David of Port Glasgow,
      41
John and Hester, 8
John Weter, 104
Jolly Tar, 97
Joseph of Dundee, 39
Joseph and Ann, 58

Jupiter, 95
Katherine, 29
Kent of Whitehaven, 33, 34
La Fleur, 122, 123
La Jeune Agathe, 96
Lamb, 51
Lark, 48
Liberty, 113
Lillie of Glasgow, 43, 44
Lively of London, 100, 101, 103, 104
Lively of Massachusetts, 96
Lively of Newburyport, 96
Loyalty of Glasgow, 19, 24, 26, 27, 28
Lucretia, 118
Lyon, 9
Magdalen, 61
Mally of Dumfries, 106
Margaret of Leith, 20
Marjory, 49
Marshal of New London, 116
Mary, 124, 127
Mary of Inverness, 41
Mary galley of Whitehaven, 14, 15, 16
Mary of Belfast, 34, 35
Mary of Philadelphia, 46
Mary and Francis of Whitehaven, 26, 32
Matilda, 127
Mayflower of Whitehaven, 35
Mercury, 109
Merry of Newburyport, 124, 125
Miflin, 94
Minerva of Charleston, South Carolina, 89, 90
Molly of Glasgow, 73
Monmouth, 92, 93

Nabob, 104
Nancy of Leith, 98
Nanino, 38
Newbury, 94
New York, 110, 111, 112, 113
Nightingale of Whitehaven, 37, 40
Northumberland, 80
Patience, 12
Pearl of Whitehaven, 22, 30, 43
Peggy of Ayr, 118
Peggy of Whitehaven, 22, 30, 43
Pelican of Saltcoats, 47
President of Glasgow, 65, 66
Prince Charles of Lorraine, 67
Prince of Wales, 91, 92
Prosperity of Glasgow, 50
Providence of Boston, 98, 104
Providence of Liverpool, 62
Quebec of Greenock, 106, 107
Queen of Newport, 24
Queen Anne of Whitehaven, 30, 31, 32
Rae galley, 84
Rappahannock of Whitehaven, 33
Rebecca, 8
Recovery of Belfast, 121
Roanoke, 60
Roselle, 128
Royal James, 19
Royal Rover, 19
St Andrew of Glasgow, 63
St David of London or Dysart, 57
St George of Montrose, 68
Salisbury, 84
Sally, 76
Sally of Greenock, 90
Sally of Kirkcaldy, 127
Sally and Becky of Boston, 95, 107
Sara and Rebecca, 103

Star of Peterhead, 1
Swallow, 48
Tarleton of Greenock, 99
Terry, 114
Theodosia of Aberdeen, 56
Thomas of Whitehaven, 28
Thomas and Betsey of Leith, 107
Tom Lee of Baltimore, 99
Trial, 60
Tynecastle, 93, 94
Virginia merchant of Aberdeen, 12
Walmington, 72
Walter of Wairwater, 4
Wexford, 90
Wharton of Whitehaven, 43, 48
Whilling Wind, 7
William and John of Glasgow, 47
Worcester, 10